Your brain is hardwired to not be hardwired.

BRANDS TO BONDS

The Evolution of Trust in the AI Age

Daniel Cruz

Work registered by Daniel Cruz, Toronto, Canada. This book is sold on the condition that it not be loaned, rented or otherwise distributed, commercially or by any other means, in any form of binding or cover other than that in which it is published. No part of this publication may be reproduced, stored in a retrieval system, or transmitted in any form or by any means (electronic, mechanical, photocopying, recording, or otherwise) without the prior written permission of Daniel Cruz.

© 2024 Daniel Cruz - All Rights Reserved

BRANDS TO BONDS

The Evolution of Trust in the AI Age

The Good Panopticon

A few years ago, Natalie, my niece, called me to ask me advise about an essay she had to present, when she was doing her International Relations degree at Concordia University.

It was about the Panopticon.

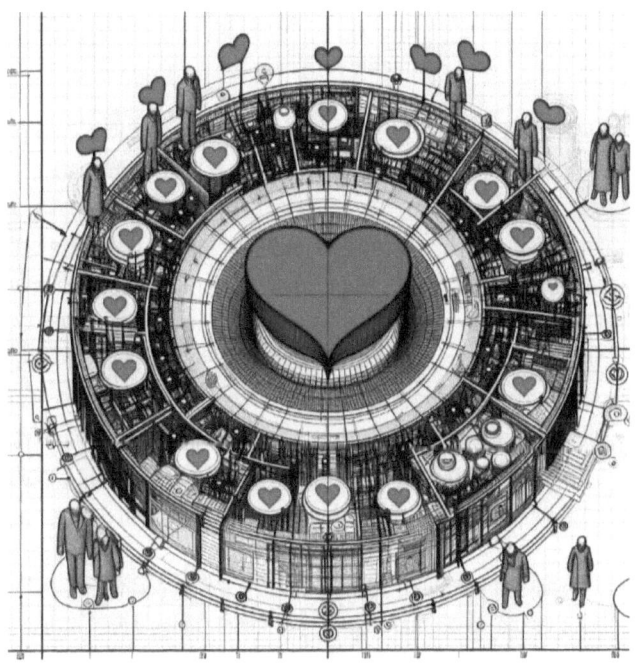

«The Building circular – an iron cage, glazed – a glass lantern about the size of Ranelagh – The Prisoners in their Cells, occupying the Circumference – The Officers, the Centre. By Blinds, and other contrivances, the Inspectors concealed from the observation of the Prisoners: hence the sentiment of a sort of invisible omnipresence.»

— *Jeremy Bentham (1791). Panopticon, or The Inspection House*

The Panopticon, conceptualized by Jeremy Bentham, is a theoretical architectural design for a prison or institution characterized by a central observation tower surrounded by cells, enabling a single observer to monitor all inmates without them knowing if they are being watched at any given moment. This design aims to induce self-discipline and control among inmates, as they internalize the possibility of constant surveillance, even when unobserved.

So!

Panopticon is a very interesting phenomenon for us who dare to dive into the behavioral sciences as applied to communication.

From what you can read, Panopticon has been perceived negatively as total surveillance concept and it has undoubtedly directed the development of surveillance technology since its very inception. Like many other negatively labeled things, I could have let go of it. But I just couldn't. For some mysterious reason I just kept getting attracted to it. Not to the surveillance part, mind you. I have never been a fan of minding what other people do with their existence, so that aspect is of no use to me.

No, it was something else. And it bothered me terribly not to be able to let go of it. There was something secret about it but I could not get it and it made me angry, a reaction compounded by the OCD present in my brain, that has a very hard time letting go of unresolved things.

In the words of Lady Galadriel, there was something *'beautiful and terrible, like the night and the morning'*, but I just could not see it.

Until I did.

I did see it.

I saw and I said:

Aren't we all panopticons anyway? Watching each other fearfully?

That's what I was intuitively perceiving. The human as panopticon. Because that is exactly what a panopticon is, the human point of view of oneself at the center of the universe.

From here, you push and create the world you wish to live in.

Again, Archimede.

And so, I fell in love with the Panopticon. Like the Beast, it became human. Like Tin Man, it got a heart.

And then, suddenly, I understood everything.

I was the Panopticon.

Myself.

That's why I had intuitively reached out in the dark for it, even not knowing why.

I was reaching for a soul.

My soul.

So...

Once I did that, I said flip it.

Use it for good.

Turn it into 'The Good Panopticon'.

Like a reverse Agent Smith, transform the panopticon and use it to turn robots into humans.

To build trust once again.

For there is high mistrust in between humans.

And that mistrust has led to separation.

This is where the technique you call BRANDING springs from.

What is branding but a simulation to artificially bridge across this mistrust?

That's the beauty of what you do, the beauty in the branding you are adept at.

It builds bridges among humans.

But as with anything human, it must evolve.

Branding is a magnificent automation, but as with anything human, it fades away.

It eventually fades away.

So, what if through The Good Panopticon you can just start to build trust again?

Advance into a new form of branding.

A branding not automated but organic.

A branding not of products but of persons.

A bridge of persons.

A personing.

Trust Acquisition

In the context of Behavioral Science, Trust Acquisition refers to the process by which individuals or entities build and cultivate trust with others. It involves establishing credibility, reliability, and integrity through consistent actions, transparent communication, and genuine interactions. Trust acquisition is essential in various contexts, including interpersonal relationships, business transactions, and societal interactions. It encompasses efforts to instill confidence, belief, and reliance in one's character, competence, and intentions, leading to mutual respect, loyalty, and cooperation. Trust Acquisition is a dynamic and ongoing process that requires time, effort, and commitment to nurture and maintain trustful relationships.

Trust

Trust is a fundamental aspect of human relationships and interactions, encompassing confidence, reliance, and belief in the integrity, reliability, and honesty of another individual, group, or entity. It involves a willingness to be vulnerable and to depend on others based on the expectation that they will act in a manner that is consistent with mutual understanding, respect, and shared values.

Key components of trust include:

- Reliability: Trust is built on the expectation that others will consistently fulfill their commitments, meet expectations, and follow through on their promises.
- Integrity: Trustworthy individuals and entities demonstrate honesty, transparency, and ethical behavior in their actions, words, and intentions.
- Consistency: Trust is reinforced through consistent behavior and communication over time, leading to a sense of predictability and stability in relationships.
- Mutual Respect: Trust involves mutual respect and consideration for the feelings, needs, and boundaries of others, fostering a sense of safety and emotional security.
- Vulnerability: Trust requires a willingness to be vulnerable and to share personal information, emotions, and experiences with others, knowing that they will be treated with care and confidentiality.
- Communication: Open, honest, and transparent communication is essential for building and maintaining trust, allowing individuals to express their thoughts, feelings, and concerns openly and to address any issues or misunderstandings.
- Empathy: Trustworthy individuals demonstrate empathy and understanding towards others, acknowledging their perspectives, emotions, and experiences with compassion and empathy.

Ultimately, trust is the foundation of healthy relationships, cooperation, and collaboration, enabling individuals and groups to work together towards common goals, resolve conflicts, and navigate challenges with confidence and mutual support.

Protocol for Transforming Branding to Personing

1. Identify the Status Quo of Your Audience

Before implementing Personing, it's crucial to understand the current state of your audience and their relationship with your brand. This includes recognizing their pain points, needs, and how they perceive your brand in the current branding paradigm. Here's how to identify the "before":

- **Analyze Customer Feedback:** Collect and review feedback from customers to understand their current experiences and frustrations with your brand.
- **Assess Engagement Levels:** Measure how engaged your audience is with your brand through metrics such as social media interactions, customer service inquiries, and repeat purchase rates.
- **Evaluate Brand Perception:** Conduct surveys and focus groups to gauge how your brand is perceived in terms of authenticity, trustworthiness, and emotional connection.

2. Define the After Personing to Your Audience

The transformation goal is to shift your audience's perception and interaction with your brand from a transactional to a relational approach. Here's what the "after" looks like:

- **Enhanced Trust and Loyalty:** Customers feel a deep sense of trust and loyalty towards your brand, seeing it as a champion of their needs and values.

- **Active Engagement:** Customers actively engage with your brand, providing feedback, participating in community activities, and feeling like integral members of the brand community.
- **Personalized Experience:** Customers experience highly personalized interactions that make them feel understood, valued, and connected.

3. Implement the 3 Core Steps to Transform into Personing

To achieve this transformation, focus on three core steps: Authentic Connection, Continuous Engagement, and Transparent Communication.

Authentic Connection

1. **Develop Higher Emotional Intelligence**
2. **Personalize Interactions**
3. **Foster Human Touch**

Continuous Engagement

1. **Create Interactive Platforms**
2. **Encourage Customer Participation**
3. **Build Community Programs**

Transparent Communication

1. **Open Information Channels**
2. **Institute Ethical Practices**
3. **Provide Responsive Support**

«In the beginning was the Word, and the Word was with God, and the Word was God»

John 1:1

Introduction

In the mystery of human interaction, **trust** has long been the elusive thread that weaves relationships, government, commerce, and society.

Throughout modern commercial history, brands have stood as heralds, representing products and services with carefully crafted identities meant to captivate and persuade.

But as the sands of time shift, so too does the nature of trust.

Yet we have arrived to the AI age, where algorithms hum with machine precision and artificial intelligence orchestrates our daily lives,

Here, a profound transformation is underway.

We stand at the cusp of a revolution where trust, once bestowed upon brands, now finds a new haven in the human connection.

This evolution is not just a paradigm shift; it's a seismic recalibration:

From Brands to Bonds.

Thus, I welcome you to "Brands to Bonds: The Evolution of Trust in the AI Age."

In the following pages, we embark on a journey that traverses the landscapes of social behavior, branding, and knowledge management.

This is not merely a narrative of change; it's an exploration of a burgeoning era where trust isn't a commodity bestowed by polished marketing campaigns but an intimate bond nurtured through authentic human connections.

Navigating the Terrain

Our exploration begins by dissecting the foundations of social behavior — the intricate dance of human interaction that has shaped civilizations.

From the nuances of communication to the psychology of trust, we delve into the intricacies that govern our relationships.

Turning the page, we encounter the realm of branding, once the vanguard of trust acquisition.

We scrutinize its constructs, unraveling the carefully spun narratives that have, for so long, dictated our preferences and loyalties.

The stage is set for a departure from the artificial gloss of branding into the uncharted territory of *Personing*.

The Rise of Personing

Personing, as we will come to understand, is more than a concept; it's a philosophy that champions authenticity, transparency, and genuine connection.

As artificial intelligence takes the reins in managing the mechanical aspects of our lives, we witness a yearning for the human touch — a trust interface that transcends the binary code.

Our journey doesn't end there.

We traverse the landscapes of knowledge management, where the transfer of information is not a transaction but a gift.

The power dynamics shift, and knowledge becomes the currency through which trust is exchanged.

Educators on social skills become the architects of this new trust economy, guiding us towards a future where empowerment is the cornerstone of every interaction.

Relevant. Or not.

"Brands to Bonds" is not a mere observation; it's a harbinger of power.

For those experts offering products and services on social networks, the terrain is changing.

The algorithms may define visibility, but it's the human touch that defines influence.

As we turn the pages of this narrative, let us not merely read but absorb the essence of *Personing* — a philosophy that transforms transactions into relationships, and relationships into enduring bonds.

Join us as we navigate the evolution of trust, from the ostentatious world of Brands to the profound simplicity of Bonds.

The journey is both introspective and forward-looking, challenging the status quo and illuminating a path towards a future where trust is not just acquired but forged in the crucible of genuine human connection.

But before we delve into the complexities, let's take a moment to lighten up with a fantastic tale from the annals of social history.

Cantinflas

The year was 1952, and Cantinflas, Mexico's beloved idol, stood before a conference room brimming with bewildered executives.

They'd hired him to revitalize the public perception of *"Almacenes Imperio"*, Mexico's greatest department store.

Data was showing that, after decades of leading the market, it was finally drowning in blandness in the middle of fierce competition.

Cantinflas, mustachioed and mischievous, surveyed the room, his eyes twinkling like chiles on a fiesta plate.

"Amigos," he began, his voice a whirlwind of Spanish and gibberish, "Almacenes Imperio is like...well, like a movie without tears! An ambiance so beige, it could put a siesta to sleep! It needs drama, passion, mambo!"

He whipped out a pair of maracas, and out of nowhere a guy popped into view with a guitar that he started playing.

Cantinflas started singing a little spontaneous song about the joys of going to a marketplace in the morning.

The executives exchanged nervous glances. Was this madman their savior? Cantinflas, oblivious, continued his charade.

He sang of the living colors of the fiesta spirit, each word punctuated by an outrageous gesture.

The room, initially skeptical, slowly began to sway. And an entire row of serious, grey marketing executives, began to write down furious notes.

No one went to sleep that night. All staff worked straight through, until morning.

The next day, a new Almacenes Imperio emerged.

The aisles were ablaze with fiery colors, with a mambo and danzón music pouring from the speakers. Pure Cantinflas poetry, promising an adventurous journey.

The campaign was Cantinflas himself, dressed as store mariachi, hosting pasarelas, offering drinks, serenading shoppers, his infectious enthusiasm a red salsa wave that swept through television news all over Mexico.

Sales soared.

Almacenes Imperio became synonymous with joy, a brand that wasn't just selling things, but a fantastic experience.

The grey executives, once bewildered, now marveled at the maestro's magic.

He hadn't just changed a brand; he'd reminded them that emotions, laughter, and a touch of the absurd can be the most potent marketing tools.

Why? Because those are the very things that make us human.

Now, I know that right now you will google *Almacenes Imperio* to check them out, right?

But don't worry, so far that department store has existed only in my mind, and hopefully you can take over from there and keep it at hand whenever you need to send your mind to fool around the aisles to find Cantinflas inspiring those around him.

As we embark on this exploration of social behavior, let's keep Cantinflas' spirit alive — a reminder that amidst the intricacies and theories, there's an innate joy and laughter in the way we connect with one another.

Joy and a bit of kinesthetics will literally take you anywhere in the world.

So, grab your maracas and let's swing into the heart of what makes us tick socially, setting the stage for understanding the very foundations upon which trust is built.

Let the exploration begin at once.

-Daniel

Contents

1. **Foundations of Social Behavior – 1**
   - Symphony of Human Communication
   - The Dynamics of Human Interaction
   - The Heart in Communication
   - The Psychology of Trust
   - Communication in the Digital Age
2. **Unraveling Branding Constructs – 23**
   - The Artifice of Brand Identities
   - The Persuasion Paradox
   - The Shifting Sands of Consumer Loyalty
3. **Enter Personing: A New Philosophy of Trust – 43**
   - Defining Personing, the whole range of nuanced, specific, heart-beat centric, human brain powered frequencies and tones that AI may imitate but never replicate.
   - Authenticity as the Cornerstone
   - Transparency in Communication
4. **Human Trust Interface - 61**
   - Beyond Binary: The Role of AI
   - The Nuances of Emotional Intelligence

- Real-Time Responsiveness
5. **Knowledge Management in the Personing Era – 79**
    - Knowledge as Currency
    - Empowering Through Information
    - The Educator's Role in the Trust Economy
6. **The Personing Revolution – 95**
    - Case Studies in Personing Success
    - Overcoming Challenges in Transition
    - Lessons from Early Adopters
7. **Building Bonds in the Digital Age – 115**
    - Community Building Through Personing
    - Adapting to Change and Feedback
    - Dynamic Relationships Over Time
8. **The Future of Trust: Personing as a Blueprint – 135**
    - Personing and the Evolving Landscape
    - Emerging Trends in Human-Centric Commerce
    - Predictions for the Next Decade
9. **Forging Enduring Bonds – 157**
    - Recapitulation of Key Concepts
    - The Imperative of Personing
    - A Clarion Call to Trust-Focused Professionals

Cognitive Overload

Cognitive overload refers to a condition in which an individual's cognitive capacity is overwhelmed by the volume or complexity of information being processed. It occurs when the brain is inundated with more information than it can effectively manage, leading to difficulties in decision-making, problem-solving, and information retention. Cognitive overload can result from various factors, including multitasking, excessive stimuli, conflicting demands, or the need to process unfamiliar or complex information. Symptoms of cognitive overload may include feelings of confusion, frustration, mental fatigue, decreased attention span, and impaired performance.

1

Foundations of Social Behavior

When we sit in the grand theater of human interaction, where the curtains rise on the drama of relationships and the comedy of misunderstandings, we find ourselves at the heart of what makes us undeniably human: *social behavior*.

Picture this—imagine a bustling ancient marketplace, where vendors vie for attention, storytellers captivate with their tales, and the exchange of goods is accompanied by the vibrant symphony of laughter and chatter.

Now, fast forward to the digital age, where the marketplace has transformed into a vast network of interconnected screens, and the storytellers have become influencers with global reach. The dynamics might have evolved, but the essence remains the same — the intricate dance of social behavior.

So, let us embark on a journey to uncover the *Foundations of Social Behavior*.

We'll delve into the psychology that underpins our interactions, explore the subtle nuances of communication, and navigate the intricate web of trust that binds us together in this digital agora.

First, the mechanics involved.

The Symphony of Human Communication

It's true, communication is a rich tapestry woven from far more than spoken words and hand gestures. Drawing from neural, behavioral, and communication sciences, let's dive into the orchestra of human elements and frequencies that create our interactions:

The Nonverbal Orchestra

- Visual: Facial expressions, eye contact, posture, clothing, and even subtle micro-expressions like eyebrow raises convey volumes about emotions, intentions, and social cues.
- Tactile: Touch plays a powerful role, from a comforting hand on the shoulder to a playful nudge, shaping intimacy, trust, and understanding.
- Auditory: Tone of voice, pitch, and even non-verbal sounds like sighs or laughter carry emotional nuance and meaning beyond the spoken word.
- Spatial: Physical proximity, the use of personal space, and even eye gaze patterns communicate comfort, dominance, and social dynamics.

The Symphony of Senses

- Olfactory: Scents can trigger powerful memories and emotions, influencing mood, attraction, and even perception.
- Gustatory: Shared meals and taste experiences can foster connection and build rapport.

The Neural Soundtrack

- Mirror Neurons: These brain cells fire both when we perform an action and when we observe someone else doing it, creating a sense of empathy and understanding.
- Limbic System: This emotional hub of the brain processes and responds to nonverbal cues, shaping our emotional reactions and communication.
- Neurotransmitters: Dopamine, oxytocin, and serotonin, released during interactions, influence trust, bonding, and positive communication.
- The Baader-Meinhof Phenomenon: Have you ever learned a new word or heard about a new concept, only to start seeing it everywhere? That's the Baader-Meinhof phenomenon, also known as frequency illusion.

The Frequencies of Communication

- Ultrasonic and Infrasonic: While inaudible to our ears, these frequencies can subconsciously influence mood and behavior.
- Body Language Frequencies: Subtle shifts in posture, gestures, and even breathing rate can communicate hidden emotions or intentions.
- Cultural Frequencies: Every culture has its own unspoken communication norms and expectations, requiring mindful adaptation.

Intention and Context

The human element remains the conductor of this communication symphony.

Our intentions, cultural background, and personal experiences shape how we interpret and send nonverbal cues. Understanding this context is crucial for effective communication.

Therefore, always remember:

Communication is a complex dance; a multi-sensory experience where words and visuals are just instruments in a vast orchestra.

By understanding the full range of human elements and frequencies at play, we can become more attuned to the unspoken and truly connect with others on a deeper level.

The Dynamics of Human Interaction

In the grand tapestry of human existence, woven with threads of emotion, intention, and connection, the dynamics of our interactions create the vibrant patterns that define our relationships.

Imagine this as a choreography, a dance where every step, every gesture, is a note in the symphony of communication.

At the heart of this dance lies a fundamental truth: we are social beings wired for connection.

Our interactions are not mere transactions; they are the currency of our shared humanity. Whether it's a warm smile that transcends language, a shared laugh that bridges cultural gaps, or a comforting touch that communicates empathy, the dynamics of human interaction are the very essence of our existence.

The Dance of Nonverbal Communication

Step onto the floor, and you'll find that much of our communication is nonverbal.

The subtle tilt of the head, the twinkle in the eye, or the gentle touch of a hand—these are the unspoken languages that convey trust, sincerity, and understanding.

In a digital world, emojis and GIFs may have joined the dance, but the essence of nonverbal communication remains a powerful force in shaping our perceptions and connections.

The Rhythm of Verbal Exchange

Words, like notes in a melody, carry the power to inspire, console, and connect.

The rhythm of verbal exchange is a delicate dance of speaking and listening.

It's not just about the words we choose but the cadence, tone, and nuance that accompany them. In a world of tweets and soundbites, understanding the importance of thoughtful, meaningful dialogue becomes crucial in fostering genuine connections.

The Harmony of Shared Experiences

You are invited to a community feast where stories are shared, experiences are recounted, and a collective narrative emerges.

The harmony of shared experiences forms the backbone of human connection. In the digital realm, this could be a shared meme that sparks laughter, a hashtag that unites a community, or a viral moment that becomes a shared memory.

These shared experiences weave a tapestry of connection that transcends physical boundaries.

As we navigate the dance floor of human interaction, let's not just focus on the individual steps but appreciate the rhythm, the harmony, and the collective beauty that emerges.

It is within this dance that trust finds its footing, creating a symphony of connections that resonate far beyond the immediate moment. In the next sections, we'll delve into the psychology that underpins these dynamics, unraveling the mysteries of why and how we come together in this intricate dance of human interaction.

But first let's check out what the heart says...

The Heart in Communication

Yes, there are growing investigations exploring the role of the heart in human communication, and it truly is fascinating territory!

Here are two main perspectives:

Heart's Influence on Communication

- *Emotional authenticity:* Our emotions, largely influenced by the heart's rhythms, can add authenticity and depth to our communication. Speaking "from the heart" can resonate with others and build trust. Studies suggest heart coherence (balanced heart rate variability) leads to clearer communication and better connection.
- *Nonverbal cues*: The heart rate, tone of voice, facial expressions, and gestures can all be subconsciously influenced by emotions and the heart's activity. These nonverbal cues can convey hidden messages and impact how our words are received.

But what's a heart without a brain?

Heart to Brain Communication

Research shows the heart is not just a passive receiver of brain signals. It has its own complex nervous system and communicates back to the brain through various channels:

- Neurologically: sending nerve impulses.
- Biochemically: releasing hormones and neurotransmitters.
- Biophysically: sending pressure waves through the bloodstream.
- Energetically: generating electromagnetic fields

Impact on decision-making and perception

This two-way communication loop influences our emotional state, decision-making, and even perception of others.

Some studies suggest heart coherence can improve cognitive function and emotional regulation. It's important to note that research in this area is still young and evolving. While some studies show intriguing connections, more work is needed to fully understand the mechanisms at play and the precise role of the heart in communication.

However, these investigations open up exciting possibilities for improving communication effectiveness by considering the heart's role.

Techniques like mindfulness and heart coherence training are being explored to help people communicate more authentically and connect with others on a deeper level.

The Psychology of Trust

Trust, that intangible currency of human connection, is a complex tapestry woven from the threads of psychology, perception, and shared experiences.

It's a delicate dance between vulnerability and assurance, where the human mind navigates a myriad of cues to determine who is worthy of faith.

The Cognitive Dance

Picture the brain as a grand ballroom, where thoughts twirl like graceful dancers. When it comes to trust, cognitive processes take center stage.

Our brains are finely tuned to assess reliability, competence, and benevolence—the trifecta that forms the foundation of trust.

From the instinctive judgments made in a split second to the more deliberate evaluations over time, the cognitive dance of trust is intricate and nuanced.

The Role of Emotional Intelligence

Step into the realm of emotional intelligence, the empathetic partner in the dance of trust.

Understanding and managing not only our emotions but also discerning the feelings of others is a key component of building trust.

It's the ability to read between the lines, perceive nonverbal cues, and respond with empathy that elevates trust from a rational decision to an emotional connection.

The Influence of Past Experiences

As we twirl through the dance of trust, our past experiences take center stage, casting a shadow or a glow on our perceptions.

Previous interactions, positive or negative, shape the lens through which we view new relationships.

Trust, in many ways, is a product of our accumulated experiences, and understanding this dance requires acknowledging the ghosts of relationships past.

Building Bridges with Consistency

Trust is not a one-time waltz; it's a continuous, evolving dance.

Consistency becomes the rhythm that bridges the steps of the cognitive dance, emotional intelligence, and past experiences.

Reliability in actions, congruence in words, and a history of dependable behavior form the melody that echoes through the corridors of trust, building a bridge from one interaction to the next.

Navigating the Dance Floor of Uncertainty

In the dance of trust, uncertainty is a partner that never leaves our side.

Navigating the unknown requires a delicate balance of openness and caution. It's an acknowledgment that trust is not a guarantee but a willingness to take the next step, even when the outcome is uncertain.

As we explore the psychology of trust, let's recognize that this dance is not scripted; it's an improvisation where every move is a response to the music of human connection.

Therefore, we must delve into the ways this psychology intersects with the dynamics of human interaction, forming the intricate patterns that shape our relationships and lead us towards the evolution from *Brands to Bonds*.

Communication in the AI Age

In the symphony of human interaction, the digital age has introduced a new movement, a dynamic crescendo of pixels and algorithms that shape the way we communicate.

As we navigate this digital dance floor, the rules have evolved, the tempo has quickened, and the stage has expanded to a global arena.

The Rise of the AI Conversation

Our daily conversation is a virtual roundtable where voices from every corner of the world converge.

In the AI age, communication has transcended physical barriers, creating a space where conversations unfold in real-time across continents.

Social media platforms, messaging apps, and virtual spaces have become the arenas where opinions are voiced, stories are shared, and connections are formed.

The Language of Emojis and Memes

Step into the world of emojis and memes, the modern hieroglyphics of the AI era.

In a landscape where attention spans are fleeting and messages must be concise, these visual cues add layers of complex expression to our digital conversations.

A well-timed emoji or a humorous meme can bridge gaps, convey emotions, and create shared experiences in the blink of an eye.

Navigating the Sea of Information

In this age of information abundance, navigating the sea of content requires a discerning eye.

From news articles to user-generated content, we are bombarded with a constant influx of information.

The ability to sift through the noise, critically evaluate sources, and engage in meaningful discussions becomes essential in fostering trust in the digital realm.

The Influence of Algorithms on Communication

As we dance through the digital landscape, AI algorithms quietly guide our steps.

Social media algorithms curate our feeds, search engine algorithms shape our discoveries, and recommendation algorithms influence our choices.

Understanding the subtle choreography of these algorithms is key to comprehending how information is disseminated, opinions are formed, and trust is built in the virtual sphere.

The Challenge of Authenticity in a Filtered World

In a world where filters can beautify reality and curated profiles present polished personas, the challenge of authenticity becomes paramount.

Navigating the digital dance floor requires a discerning audience that can differentiate between curated narratives and genuine, unfiltered expressions. Authenticity, in this context, becomes the linchpin of trust in the digital age.

The Art of Digital Listening

In the midst of the digital cacophony, the art of digital listening emerges as a crucial skill. Active engagement, responsiveness, and a genuine interest in the perspectives of others create a harmonious dialogue.

The dance of digital communication is not just about speaking; it's about listening, understanding, and responding in a way that fosters connection and builds trust. As we explore the nuances of communication in the digital age, let's remember that behind every pixelated message is a human voice seeking connection.

In the chapters that follow, we'll delve deeper into how these digital dynamics intersect with the psychology of trust, paving the way for a profound evolution *from Brands to Bonds in the AI age.*

Who would've thought that one day we'd be relying on algorithms to make us laugh and help us navigate the complexities of human interaction?

It's like the universe decided to play a cosmic joke on us, and we're all just along for the ride.

So, let's raise a glass to the AI overlords and hope they keep the punchlines coming, because in this age of artificial intelligence, laughter truly is the best medicine.

Brands to Bonds

Branding As Automation

Branding operates as an automation of the opening stage of communication by serving as a shorthand method for conveying information about a product, service, or company to consumers. It essentially acts as a visual and conceptual cue that triggers associations, emotions, and expectations in the minds of individuals. By automating the opening stage of communication, branding allows companies and individuals to convey key messages about their values, offerings, and unique selling propositions without the need for lengthy explanations or interactions.

Brands to Bonds

Brands to Bonds

2

Unraveling Branding Constructs

In the grand tapestry of human behavior, branding stands as a curious fabric—an intricate blend of psychology, sociology, and a touch of artistry.

As we delve into the heart of *Unraveling Branding Constructs*, let's approach it with the spirit of a social scientist donning a detective's hat, ready to unravel the mysteries behind the logos, slogans, and carefully crafted narratives.

Imagine entering the world of a renowned anthropologist who, armed with nothing but a notebook and an insatiable curiosity, ventured into a bustling marketplace.

This scientist wasn't hunting for fossils or ancient artifacts; they were on a quest to decode the cultural artifacts of their time—the brands that adorned storefronts and market stalls.

In the spirit of this intrepid investigator, let's embark on our own journey to unravel the enigmatic world of branding.

Picture us as modern anthropologists navigating the jungles of consumer culture, armed not with machetes but with an understanding that behind every logo lies a story, and within every slogan, a whispered promise.

Now, for a lighthearted touch, let's take a moment to share an anecdote from the annals of social science.

Consider the tale of *Dr. Amelia Beacon*, a witty social psychologist who, 50 years ago, in her quest to understand the allure of brands, once conducted a peculiar experiment.

Dr. Beacon, wisely armed with a group of unsuspecting participants, set out to measure the emotional responses triggered by famous logos.

The results were both amusing and enlightening, as participants exhibited a range of emotions from nostalgia to downright hilarity when confronted with the symbols of their beloved and celebrated favorite brands.

Yet if you repeat the same experiment today, the results will be much less impressive.

And we must ask ourselves why.

So, with a nod to Dr. Beacon's playful exploration and the spirit of anthropological curiosity, let's embark on our own journey of Unraveling Branding Constructs. In the sections that follow, we'll dissect the artifice of brand identities, explore the paradox of persuasion, and navigate the shifting sands of consumer loyalty.

It's a journey into the heart of human behavior, where brands are not just products on shelves but cultural artifacts that reflect the intricate dance between commerce and psychology.

The Artifice of Brand Identities

The elaborate theater of consumer culture has brand identities taking center stage, adorned with carefully chosen colors, sleek logos, and promises of a better, trendier, or more fulfilling life. However, beneath this façade lies a sleek paradox—the assumption that a brand gains legitimacy simply because consumers, in their trust, take it at face value.

The fatal flaw?

The unspoken agreement that consumers won't protest the artificial nature of the construct.

In fact, we do.

Silently we despise the mediocrity of all brands and laugh at all of you idiots whom take us for fools, just because whatever crap you sell happened to be of convenience to us.

The Mirage of Legitimacy

Brands, in their quest for market share, often craft identities akin to shimmering mirages in the desert of consumer choices.

The colors are vibrant, the promises are alluring, and the imagery is meticulously chosen.

Yet, in this mirage, there's a hidden assumption—that the perceived legitimacy bestowed by the brand's external appearance is enough to secure trust.

It's an assumption that consumers, lulled by the visual symphony of branding, won't lift the curtain to reveal the mechanisms behind the scenes.

In fact, we do.

Though we already know your tricks and they have become so boring, so lacking, that there's no longer any need to lift any curtain.

Hell, we no longer give any thought to the fact that we know you are ripping us of, charging us precious money just *'for perception'*, right?

We know you know.

And you know we know you know.

The Power of Perception

The artifice of brand identities relies heavily on the power of perception.

A well-designed logo, a catchy slogan, and a compelling narrative can create an illusion of authenticity.

However, this perception is not an intrinsic truth; it's a construct carefully designed to evoke specific emotions and associations.

The fatal flaw emerges when brands overestimate the longevity of this illusion without addressing the evolving consciousness of consumers.

The Fatal Flaw: Consumer Silence

Herein lies the Achilles' heel of brand identity—the often-unspoken acceptance by consumers.

The fatal flaw is not that brands construct artificial identities; it's the assumption that consumers, even when aware of the artifice, will remain silent.

Consumer silence does not equate to endorsement.

It's a precarious peace that can shatter when trust is tested.

The assumption that brand legitimacy is a given, even in the face of consumer awareness, is the keystone that, when dislodged, brings down the entire arch of brand identity.

Navigating Beyond the Mirage

To unravel the artifice of brand identities, we must navigate beyond the mirage.

It involves questioning assumptions, lifting the veil of perception, and fostering a culture where consumers feel empowered to challenge the artificial nature of branding.

The fatal flaw can be mitigated through open dialogue, transparency, and a willingness to acknowledge that the authenticity of a brand is not a static entity—it's a living, breathing relationship between the brand and its consumers.

As we navigate this landscape, let's not only examine the intricacies of brand construction but also encourage a discourse where consumer voices are not suppressed by the allure of logos or the gloss of marketing narratives.

It's a journey beyond the mirage, where the fatal flaw is transformed into an opportunity for brands to embrace genuine authenticity and build trust through transparency.

The Persuasion Paradox

In the realm of branding, the siren song of persuasion has long been the melody that lures consumers into the fold.

Yet, within this melody lies a paradox, a psychological quirk that challenges the very foundation of short-term persuasion and its lasting impact on consumer behavior.

Enter the *Persuasion Paradox*—a theory introduced by psychologist Robert Cialdini in 1984, and as we unravel its layers, we find that it reflects a fascinating allergic reaction against the artificial elements embedded in face value persuasion.

The Short-Term Allure

In the short term, the art of persuasion is akin to a captivating dance.

Brands employ a repertoire of tactics—enticing visuals, compelling narratives, and carefully crafted messaging—all designed to captivate the audience and prompt immediate action.

The allure is undeniable, and consumers often find themselves swayed by the symphony of persuasive elements.

The Unraveling Tapestry

However, as we step into the paradox, we encounter a fascinating phenomenon.

The greater the initial persuasion, the more intricate the unraveling of the tapestry in the long term.

What initially appears as a seamless, persuasive construct begins to show signs of wear as consumers navigate beyond the immediate appeal.

It's as if the artificial elements used in short-term persuasion trigger a psychological allergic reaction—a subtle resistance against the very tactics that once held sway.

The brain does not like artificial hardwiring.

Consumer Perception Evolution

The Persuasion Paradox is not a mere quirk; it's a reflection of the evolution of consumer perception.

The artificial elements that initially induce compliance become the seeds of skepticism when the long-term relationship is considered.

Consumers, in their evolving awareness, develop a resistance to persuasion that lacks authenticity.

The very elements that once captured attention become the targets of scrutiny as the consumer's perception matures.

Building Trust Beyond Persuasion

To navigate the Persuasion Paradox, brands must recognize that the allure of short-term persuasion may not translate into enduring trust.

Instead, the focus shifts towards building authentic connections that withstand the test of time.

Trust is not a byproduct of immediate compliance; it's a slow-burning flame that requires the steady fuel of transparency, honesty, and a genuine commitment to the consumer relationship.

The Challenge of a Balancing Act

The Persuasion Paradox presents a challenge—a delicate balancing act between immediate impact and lasting influence.

Brands must tread carefully, understanding that while short-term persuasion can spark interest, it's the long-term authenticity that forges enduring connections.

The unraveling tapestry of the Persuasion Paradox invites brands to step beyond the confines of artificial constructs and embrace the genuine, even when faced with the paradoxical nature of consumer persuasion.

In the sections to follow, we'll explore how brands can navigate this paradox and transition from short-term allure to the cultivation of trust that withstands the test of time in the age of Personing.

The Shifting Sands of Consumer Loyalty

In the landscape of consumer loyalty, the foundations of all brands are built on the shifting sands of trust—a trust that, when artificially constructed, faces an inevitable decay over time.

As we trace the journey from the allure of short-term persuasion to the unraveling tapestry of the Persuasion Paradox, we find ourselves standing at the crossroads where traditional branding, with its reliance on face value persuasion, faces the unavoidable phasing out in the age of Personing.

The Ephemeral Nature of Trust

Consumer loyalty, when founded on the ephemeral nature of short-term persuasion, resembles a sandcastle standing tall against the tide.

The initial trust, built upon the allure of branding elements, begins to erode as the consumer perception evolves. The very elements that once captivated become mere grains in the shifting sands of changing preferences and heightened awareness.

The Decay of Initial Trust

The Persuasion Paradox acts as an accelerant in the decay of initial trust.

What once seemed robust and unassailable starts to show cracks as consumers, armed with an evolving awareness, begin to question the authenticity of the persuasive constructs.

The decay is not a reflection of consumer fickleness but a natural response to the artificial elements woven into the initial trust-building process.

The Unraveling Tapestry's Impact on Loyalty

As the tapestry unravels, so does the foundation of consumer loyalty built on the illusions of branding.

Loyalty is not a static state; it's a dynamic relationship that requires a continuous exchange of trust. When that trust is built on artificial constructs, the erosion becomes inevitable.

The sands shift, and consumer loyalty transitions from a foundation of compliance to a quest for authentic connections.

The Rise of Personing

Enter Personing—a paradigm shift that acknowledges the inevitable decay of traditional branding.

Personing embraces the understanding that trust is not a one-time transaction but a continuous dance between authenticity and consumer perception.

It recognizes that the shifting sands of loyalty can be stabilized when the foundation is built on genuine human connections, transparent communication, and a commitment to fostering trust that withstands the test of time.

The Unavoidable Phasing Out

In the age of Personing, the phasing out of traditional branding becomes an unavoidable reality.

The artificial constructs that once propped up consumer loyalty are replaced by the enduring pillars of human-to-human communication, authenticity, and a commitment to knowledge sharing.

Check out Maslow's Pyramid of human needs.

Brands that resist this transition find themselves stranded on eroding shores, while those that embrace Personing navigate the shifting sands with resilience and agility.

As we explore the inevitable phasing out of traditional branding, let's recognize that the decay of initial trust is not a downfall but an opportunity—an opportunity for brands to transcend the limitations of face value persuasion and build relationships that endure in the evolving landscape of consumer loyalty.

All in all, it seems like the world of branding has been going through a bit of a midlife crisis lately.

We've got logos morphing like Pokémon, companies rebranding to single letters like they're trying to win a game of Scrabble, and a whole lot of identity crises happening left and right.

It's like watching a sitcom where the main character keeps changing their outfit, hoping to find the perfect look, only to realize they've been wearing a lampshade on their head the whole time. And let's not forget the poor performance marketers, who are probably sitting in a corner, shaking their heads and muttering, *"I told you so."*

But hey, at least we're all learning that a pretty logo doesn't make a brand. It's like trying to put lipstick on a pig and expecting it to win a beauty pageant.

Spoiler alert: it won't.

So here's to hoping that brands finally realize that it's what's on the inside that counts, and maybe we'll see a bit more substance and a little less fluff in the branding world.

Just put more heart salsa in it, ma'am.

Brands to Bonds

Heart Communication

Heart communication refers to a form of interpersonal interaction that transcends mere words or gestures, instead connecting individuals on a deeper emotional level. It involves the exchange of genuine emotions, empathy, and understanding between people, fostering a sense of closeness, trust, and mutual respect.

Unlike conventional communication, which often focuses on conveying information or ideas, heart communication emphasizes the expression and reception of feelings, intentions, and vulnerabilities. It involves active listening, compassion, and openness to the emotional experiences of others, creating a safe space for authentic expression and connection.

Heart communication is characterized by sincerity, vulnerability, and empathy, as individuals share their true thoughts and emotions without fear of judgment or rejection. It allows for deep bonds to form between people, enriching relationships and enhancing overall well-being.

Brands to Bonds

Brands to Bonds

3

Enter Personing: A New Philosophy of Trust

Welcome to the dawn of a transformative era, where the old guard of post-sales activities and transactional relationships gives way to a new philosophy that transcends the transactional into the transformational.

Personing isn't just a concept; it's a philosophy that recognizes the limitations of the post-sales era, shedding the decaying paradigm of customer service and support that lingers on the outer shell of human relations.

The Evolution Beyond Transactions

Personing beckons us to step beyond the confines of transactional relationships.

In the annals of behavioral science and neural language programming, we find the evidence that the post-sales era, tethered to activities like customer support and warranty services, has reached its zenith.

The evolution beyond transactions is not just a call for change; it's a beckoning towards a deeper understanding of what it means to build trust in the human experience.

The transactional will always be there, but it will be built upon towards a transformational experience.

The Decay of the Transactional

The paradigm of post-sales activities, while once a beacon of customer-centricity, has begun to show signs of decay.

Customer support hotlines and follow-up emails, while functional, exist on the periphery of human connection.

And that is why it is being automated.

Personing recognizes that true trust is not built through scripted conversations and automated responses but through genuine, human-to-human engagement that permeates the core of relationships.

Redefining the Customer-Brand Dynamic

Personing is an instructional guide that invites brands to redefine the customer-brand dynamic.

In the neural language of programming, it understands that the script of post-sales interactions, no matter how well-crafted, falls short of creating the neural pathways associated with genuine trust.

It's a motivational journey towards a paradigm where every interaction is an opportunity to forge a lasting bond, transcending the transactional to the relational.

As we enter the realm of Personing, let's leave behind the relics of post-sales activities and embrace a new philosophy that transforms transactions into connections.

In the chapters ahead, we'll explore the intricacies of Personing—defining it, understanding its nuances, and unlocking the potential for brands to become not just providers of products and services but architects of trust in the evolving landscape of human relations.

Get ready to embark on a journey where transactions are replaced by connections, and relationships are not just built but *personed*.

Defining Personing

In the symphony of human interaction, Personing emerges as the virtuoso performance, transcending the scripted melodies of traditional post-sales activities.

It's more than a concept; it's a profound shift in the way brands and individuals engage, recognizing the limitations of artificial intelligence in replicating the nuanced, specific, heart-beat centric frequencies that define the human trust-building process.

Behavioral Models and Trust Building

Personing draws inspiration from behavioral models that underscore the intricacies of human behavior.

It understands that trust isn't a linear equation solved by scripted responses but a dynamic interplay influenced by a myriad of factors. Behavioral models in psychology emphasize the importance of authenticity, empathy, and emotional intelligence—key elements that form the backbone of Personing.

The Heartbeat of Communication

In the realm of communication models, Personing recognizes that the heartbeat of interaction lies in the subtleties—tones, inflections, pauses, and the genuine warmth that emanates from human conversation.

While AI may replicate words, it struggles to replicate the heartbeat centric frequencies that create a connection.

Personing is not just about what is said but how it is said, acknowledging that the power of tone and nuance is unparalleled in the trust-building process.

The Human Brain as the Ultimate Trust Interface

As we delve into the neural landscape, Personing aligns with the understanding that the human brain is the ultimate trust interface.

While AI can process information and provide solutions, it lacks the innate ability to read emotions, respond to nonverbal cues, and navigate the unspoken nuances of human interaction.

Personing leverages the power of the human brain to create connections that go beyond the transactional and forge a trust that resonates on a neural level.

Because the brain has only one original hardwiring, the one it was born with, and eventually sheds away all artifice.

The Superiority of Personing over AI Imitation

Personing stands tall as the superior force in trust building, precisely because it transcends the limitations of AI imitation.

While AI can mimic responses based on learned patterns, it cannot authentically experience emotions, understand context, or respond to the unpredictable dynamics of human interaction.

Personing is the acknowledgment that the nuances, frequencies, and tones of genuine connection are irreplaceable, creating a trust-building process that is inherently human.

Today we know that brands can leverage the principles of Personing, embracing the behavioral and communication models that define authentic human connections.

Personing isn't a replacement for technology; it's a harmonious integration that places the human at the center of trust building, recognizing that in the vast symphony of interactions, the human heartbeat remains the most resonant and trustworthy frequency.

What this means is that brands must embrace a return to full human operations on every possible level where they can be implemented.

Authenticity as the Keystone

In the age of Personing, authenticity emerges as the keystone, not as a static concept but as a dynamic, developmental process.

We transcend the notion of authenticity as a fixed state and embrace a perspective that views it as a continuous journey—a process of becoming rather than being. In this light, we introduce a new element to authenticity: continuity.

From Authenticity to Continuity

Traditionally, authenticity has been associated with uniformity—aligning one's actions with beliefs, conventionality—adhering to societal norms, and connectivity—building genuine relationships.

Now, we add continuity to the journey.

Continuity captures the developmental character of authenticity, recognizing the ever-changing relationships between individuals and themselves, others, and the evolving social norms that shape their lives.

Our brains, after all, are of a rebellious nature.

The Developmental Nature of Authenticity

Authenticity as continuity goes beyond the static view, acknowledging that authenticity is not a destination but a journey.

It embraces the inherent changes in authenticity over time, emphasizing the congruous relationship between an entity and the features of its development.

This perspective places a greater emphasis on becoming authentic, recognizing authenticity as an ongoing project that evolves with each interaction, experience, and phase of life.

Bridging Static and Process Characteristics

Authenticity as continuity becomes the bridge between static and process characteristics of authenticity.

It captures the dynamic connection between who we are and who we are becoming, fostering a holistic understanding of authenticity.

As we become, we are embrace the new and discard the old in our presence.

This perspective aligns seamlessly with the principles of Personing, where the authenticity of human connections is not confined to a singular moment but unfolds as a continuous, evolving narrative, connecting a myriad of streams of cognition.

From Being to Becoming Authentic

In the sections ahead, we'll explore how authenticity as continuity transforms the way brands engage with individuals.

It invites us to move beyond the static view of authenticity and embrace the fluid, ever-changing nature of human connections.

Personing, rooted in authenticity as continuity, becomes a journey of becoming authentic—a process that aligns with the dynamic ebb and flow of life, relationships, and the evolving landscape of trust-building in the age where connections are the currency and authenticity is the guiding star.

This is how the transactional becomes carried away into the transformational, by seamlessly fusing experiences and contemplations, realities and expectations, into a continuum.

Transparency in Communication: Embracing the Evolution

As we delve deeper into the realms of Personing, authenticity as continuity, and the dynamic nature of trust-building, we find ourselves at the crossroads of transparency in communication—a pivotal point where the traditional armor of mechanization in sales and customer relations meets the transformative power of high-performance loops.

The Low-Performance Loop

In the current landscape, brands often find solace in the low-performance loop of mechanized sales and customer relations.

The modus operandi involves reaching out to individuals to provoke sales and, post-sales, managing customer relations to encourage repeat transactions. However, this loop, once efficient, inevitably decays over time. The mechanization, while streamlined, lacks the adaptability and depth needed to foster genuine connections.

This low performance loop simply cannot develop into transformational.

Shaping the High-Performance Loop

Personing, in its essence, imposes the evolution towards a high-performance loop—one that transcends the transactional to embrace the transformational.

The heart of Personing lies in the acknowledgment that individuals are not mere users or clients but integral team members contributing to a shared narrative.

This shift reshapes the dynamics, prompting brands to react in real time to the authentic input from persons, thereby creating a continuous loop of improvement and evolution.

The Fearless Embrace of Transparency

In the journey towards Personing, transparency becomes the guiding light.

Brands must not fear the transparency that accompanies this evolution.

Instead, they must embrace it wholeheartedly.

Transparency is not a vulnerability; it's the foundation of authentic communication.

It involves laying bare the operating principles, showcasing the commitment to continuous improvement, and inviting individuals into a shared space where trust is built on openness, honesty, and a mutual understanding of evolving dynamics.

From Users/Clients to Team Members

As we unravel the layers of transparency in communication, let's envision a world where individuals transition from being mere users or clients to integral team members.

Personing is not just a shift in terminology; it's a fundamental change in perspective. Team members contribute not only to the success of a transaction but actively shape the principles and dynamics that guide the brand's evolution. Transparency becomes the bridge that connects the brand's journey with the collective narrative of its team members.

The Continuous Loop of Improvement

The high-performance loop fueled by transparency creates a continuous loop of improvement.

Brands, no longer confined to scripted responses and predetermined interactions, adapt and grow in response to the real-time input from team members.

This loop becomes the lifeblood of Personing—an ever-evolving journey where each interaction contributes to the shared narrative, shaping the brand's trajectory and fostering trust in the process.

Now, we must delve deeper into the practical applications of transparency in communication, exploring how brands can fearlessly embrace this evolution, transition from low-performance to high-performance loops, and cultivate relationships that transcend transactions in the age of Personing.

I mean, who knew that the secret to unlocking the mysteries of the universe was hiding in the subtle art of human conversation?

Imagine a world where people communicate solely through the rhythmic patterns of their heartbeats, the delicate inflections in their voices, and the well-timed pauses that leave you hanging on the edge of your seat. It's like a cosmic dance of words and emotions, where every conversation is a symphony of human connection.

But let's not forget the *pièce de résistance*: the genuine warmth that emanates from human conversation. Voice is a cozy blanket on a chilly night, wrapping you in a comforting embrace of understanding and camaraderie.

And to think, all this time we've been trying to find the meaning of life in the stars, when it was right there in our own voices, waiting to be heard.

So, the next time you find yourself lost in the labyrinth of human interaction, just remember to listen to your heart(beat), speak with a little inflection, and pause for dramatic effect.

After all, in the grand scheme of the universe, it's the little things that make all the difference.

Emotional Intelligence

Emotional intelligence refers to the ability to recognize, understand, and manage one's own emotions, as well as to perceive, interpret, and respond effectively to the emotions of others. It encompasses a range of skills and competencies, including self-awareness, self-regulation, empathy, and social skills, which enable individuals to navigate social interactions, communicate effectively, and build strong relationships. Emotional intelligence plays a crucial role in personal and professional success, as it influences how individuals perceive and manage stress, solve problems, make decisions, and collaborate with others.

Brands to Bonds

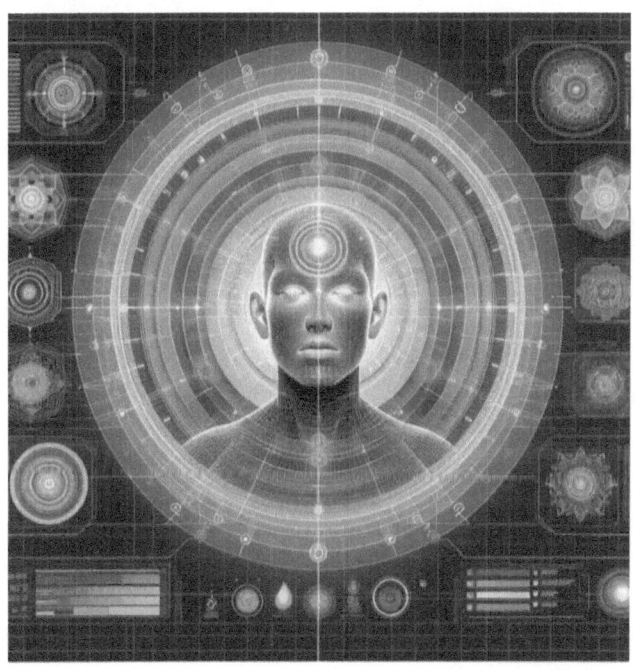

Brands to Bonds

4

Human Trust Interface

We struggle to stay afloat in the unforgiving maelstrom of contemporary consumer relationships, a groundbreaking shift is underway—an evolution from transactional encounters to the embrace of a "Human Trust Interface."

This paradigm goes beyond the traditional customer service models, which, while efficient in issue resolution, fall short in addressing the profound yearning for authentic connections in today's consumer landscape.

Challenges of the Current Approach

1. **Transactional vs. Relational:** The conventional emphasis on swiftly resolving individual problems results in transactional interactions, lacking the depth necessary for cultivating enduring customer relationships.
2. **Scripted Responses & Lack of Personalization:** Standardized responses, often employed in traditional models, can feel robotic and disconnected. Modern customers demand interactions that are personalized and emotionally resonant.

3. **One-Way Communication:** Traditional models predominantly focus on brands delivering information, creating a one-way street. In contrast, today's consumers seek open communication, active listening, and platforms to share their voices.

4. **Power Imbalance:** The conventional structure often places customer service representatives as mere problem solvers, inadvertently creating a power imbalance. Empowering customers through self-service options and collaborative problem-solving is essential in fostering trust.

5. **Lack of Transparency & Empathy:** With growing concerns about data privacy and corporate responsibility, customers expect transparency and empathy. Practices lacking transparency and dismissive attitudes quickly erode trust.

The Human Trust Interface

The "Human Trust Interface" approach addresses these challenges through a holistic strategy:

1. **Prioritizing Authentic Connections:** By placing a premium on genuine connections, brands commit to building relationships through personalized interactions and human empathy.
2. **Facilitating Two-Way Communication:** Encouraging open dialogue, active listening, and the incorporation of customer feedback, this approach transforms communication into a dynamic exchange rather than a one-sided delivery.
3. **Empowering Customers:** Recognizing the importance of empowering customers, brands provide self-service options and engage in collaborative problem-solving, fostering a sense of ownership and control.
4. **Embracing Transparency and Ethical Practices:** Trust is built through openness about data usage and a commitment to social responsibility.

Brands embracing transparency and ethical practices stand out as beacons of trustworthiness.

5. **Leveraging Technology Strategically:** While technology plays a crucial role, it is strategically employed. Tools like AI and data analysis personalize interactions and anticipate customer needs, all while maintaining human oversight and ethical implementation.

By embracing the principles of a "Human Trust Interface," brands can transcend the limitations of transactional engagements.

This shift marks a journey from solving immediate problems to cultivating relationships that stand resilient over time.

The result is increased loyalty, advocacy, and the foundation for sustained success in the ever-evolving landscape of human connections and brand relationships.

Beyond Binary: The Role of AI

In the evolving landscape of branding, Artificial Intelligence (AI) emerges as a transformative force, wielding unparalleled capabilities yet falling short in certain crucial aspects.

AI is not a silver bullet; rather, it acts as a powerful tool reshaping the way brands engage with their audience.

Its strengths lie in data analysis and personalization, enabling hyper-personalized experiences and automating repetitive tasks to free up creative capacities. AI chatbots provide 24/7 customer support, ensuring seamless interaction.

AI Limits

However, despite its strengths, AI encounters limitations when it comes to building genuine connections.

It lacks the nuanced human touch crucial for establishing authentic connections, as the emotional intelligence, empathy, and spontaneity defining human interactions remain beyond its reach.

It's imperative to view AI as a facilitator, not a replacement, for human creativity, empathy, and ethical decision-making.

A Meaningful Touch

For successful Personing in the AI age, a strategic approach is paramount. Meaningful human connections must stand above technology.

Brands should leverage the strengths of AI for data-driven personalization and efficiency while preserving the human touch in areas that require emotional intelligence, genuine empathy, and ethical decision-making.

Strategic Interaction

In essence, the synergy between AI and human elements defines the path forward. It's not a question of AI or human connection; rather, it's a strategic integration where technology enhances the brand's capabilities, allowing human creativity and empathy to shine in the pursuit of authentic relationships.

This may well mean AI as turbo thrust of authentic human connection.

The Nuances of Emotional Intelligence

In the realm of today's experience-driven world, the journey to earn trust transcends the realms of cold logic and efficiency.

Emotional Intelligence (EI) emerges as a crucial differentiator, positioned at the heart of building robust, enduring connections with your audience.

It extends beyond the transactional and allows you to delve into the intricacies of human behavior, understanding and responding to the feelings, needs, and motivations that drive it.

Understanding and Responding

Emotional intelligence empowers you to go beyond surface-level interactions. It enables a profound understanding of the emotional landscape, allowing you to respond with a level of depth that resonates with individuals on a personal level.

By acknowledging and addressing their emotional needs, you create an environment where people feel genuinely valued and respected.

Demonstrating Empathy and Active Listening

At the core of emotional intelligence lies empathy and active listening.

By demonstrating genuine concern for the emotions of your audience, you carve out a space where trust can flourish.

Active listening, coupled with empathy, establishes a foundation for meaningful connections, showcasing that you not only hear but also understand the emotional reality of those you engage with.

Navigating Challenges with Tact

Emotional intelligence comes to the forefront when navigating sensitive situations.

It equips you with the ability to approach challenges with tact and grace, mitigating negative emotions.

By handling difficulties with empathy and understanding, you not only preserve trust but also contribute to its growth during moments of adversity.

Trust, after all, is a child of transparency.

Expressing Positive Emotions Strategically

Strategic expression of positive emotions becomes a powerful tool in the arsenal of emotional intelligence.

By strategically infusing positivity into interactions, you create a sense of connection and optimism. This deliberate emotional resonance goes beyond mere transactions, solidifying trust and fostering loyalty.

Moving Beyond Meeting Needs

Ultimately, emotional intelligence propels you beyond the realm of merely meeting needs. It empowers you to resonate with your audience on a deeper, emotional level.

The trust built through emotional intelligence transcends transactional engagements, paving the way for lasting relationships and, consequently, brand success. In the landscape of Personing, connections are the currency, while emotional intelligence stands as a guiding force—a compass navigating the nuances of human emotions, fostering trust, and laying the foundation for enduring relationships that extend far beyond the realms of mere transactions.

Real-Time Responsiveness

In the evolution of brand decision-making, the reliance on crystal balls and complex algorithms is making way for the vibrant pulse of real-time human responsiveness.

This shift transcends the confines of sterile boardrooms, inviting brands to embrace the unpredictable and energetic connections forged through genuine human interactions.

Beyond Calculations, Towards Connection

Picture a world where decisions are not dictated by calculated predictions but are rather fueled by a nuanced understanding derived from real-time interactions with customers, employees, and stakeholders.

This move represents more than a passing trend; it signifies a seismic shift—a departure from calculated forecasts towards an embrace of the dynamic tapestry woven by human emotions, opinions, and experiences.

Again, this is the full human approach, which requires the renaissance of human centric organizations focusing upon perfecting the tools of human communication.

Live Feedback, Instant Adaptation

Envision a brand leader receiving live feedback on a new campaign via social media, instantly adapting messaging based on genuine reactions.

This dynamic responsiveness extends beyond marketing realms, reaching into customer service where representatives are empowered to provide real-time solutions, fostering trust and loyalty beyond scripted responses.

Speed with Substance

Real-time responsiveness isn't solely about speed; it's about tapping into the collective intelligence, empathy, and creativity that humans uniquely possess.

It's the real time integration of human insights into the decision-making fabric, ensuring brands stay agile, relevant, and deeply connected to the ever-evolving human narrative.

This while definitely require the reinvention of branding campaigns into the powerful dynamic architecture of social mobilization, reaching out to embrace the immense complexity of the human experience.

Proactively Shaping the Narrative

This approach goes beyond reacting; it's about proactively shaping the brand journey with the very essence of what makes us human: our ever-evolving stories, emotions, and shared experiences.

In the era of Personing, real-time human responsiveness becomes the cornerstone of brand excellence—a dynamic force that propels brands beyond mere financial transactions into the realm of full human connections.

Co-Creating Enduring Stories

Staying attuned to the rhythm of human experiences, brands actively participate in the ongoing narrative. It's a journey where brands and individuals co-create stories that resonate, endure, and evolve.

Real-time human responsiveness becomes not just a strategy but a philosophy—a commitment to weaving the threads of humanity into the very fabric of brand identity, ensuring that each interaction becomes a meaningful and resonant chapter in the shared story.

Through Personing, brands will finally be catching on to the fact that we're not just walking wallets waiting to be emptied.

The Human Trust Interface is the love child of a self-help book and a marketing strategy, and it's about time we all jumped on that triumphant bandwagon.

Imagine a world where brands are no longer just trying to sell you stuff, but instead, they're your best friend, your confidant, and your personal cheerleader.

But let's not forget the real prize here: loyalty, advocacy, and sustained success. It's like a brand relationship hat trick, and we're all just waiting for the confetti to fall. So, here's to hoping that brands finally realize that the key to our hearts *(and wallets)* is through genuine human connection, and not just another flashy ad campaign.

In the end, it's all about transcending the limitations of transactional engagements.

Because let's face it, we're all just looking for a little love and understanding in this crazy world, and if a brand can provide that, well, they've got our loyalty for life.

Brands to Bonds

Hero Archetype

The hero archetype is a fundamental and recurring character archetype found in myths, legends, literature, and storytelling across cultures and civilizations. The hero is typically portrayed as a brave and noble figure who embarks on a journey or quest to confront challenges, overcome obstacles, and achieve great feats. Often guided by a sense of duty, honor, or a desire to help others, the hero demonstrates courage, resilience, and self-sacrifice in the face of adversity.

Brands to Bonds

Brands to Bonds

5

Knowledge Management in the Personing Era

The grand hall of the Palace of Personing is magic laboratory where real human connections and authentic relationships take center stage, in order for knowledge management to become a pivotal element in shaping the brand narrative.

This chapter delves into the transformative power of knowledge management within the Personing era—a paradigm that empowers users as brand team members.

Unveiling the Triumph of Personing

Personing stands as a triumphant evolution in brand communication.

It goes beyond the conventional approaches of showcasing strengths and achievements.

Instead, it embraces transparency, revealing challenges and needs, fostering a genuine connection between brands and their audience.

This shift harks back to a *'defender of the people'* approach—a strategy that found success for American brands in the early 20th century.

As we explore knowledge management in the Personing era, this historical perspective serves as a foundation for understanding the potency of real-time information exchange.

Empowering Users as Brand Team Members

Personing liberates brand information from the confines of one-way communication.

It transforms users into active participants, essentially brand team members, armed with real-time information that enables them to react and support the brand when summoned.

This empowerment marks a departure from the traditional model of passive consumers to engaged collaborators—*an evolution that echoes the democratic ideals of brand engagement from a bygone era.*

Real-Time Information Exchange and Support

At the core of Personing's knowledge management is the emphasis on real-time information exchange.

Users, equipped with insights into challenges and needs, become integral to the brand's decision-making process. This real-time interaction fosters a dynamic and responsive relationship, resembling the *'defender of the people'* hero archetype.

Brands gain agility and relevance by leveraging the collective intelligence, empathy, and creativity that their user-base brings to the table. As we navigate the landscape of Personing and knowledge management, the fusion of historical successes, contemporary strategies, and future possibilities unfolds.

The empowerment of users as brand team members becomes not just a methodology but a philosophy—a commitment to a collaborative journey where information flows freely, relationships deepen authentically, and *brands evolve in tandem with the dynamic narratives of their engaged communities.*

Knowledge as Currency

In the era of Personing, knowledge becomes the invaluable currency that powers the dynamic relationship between brands and users, transforming them from passive consumers into active team members.

The precision of brand knowledge holds the key to empowering users, bringing them aboard with a real-time, high-performance information feedback loop.

Empowering Users as Active Contributors

Brand knowledge, when shared with precision, serves as an invitation for users to become active contributors to the brand narrative. In the Personing paradigm, information is not merely disseminated; it's a collaborative exchange that empowers users to understand the intricacies, challenges, and needs of the brand. This transparency invites them to step into the role of team members rather than bystanders.

Real-Time Information Feedback Loop

The power of knowledge is magnified in the real-time information feedback loop that Personing fosters. Users armed with up-to-the-moment insights into the brand's strengths, weaknesses, and evolving narrative become integral components of the decision-making process.

Their immediate feedback, driven by precise brand knowledge, transforms the brand-user relationship into a responsive, agile, and mutually beneficial partnership.

High-Performance Collaboration

Precision in brand knowledge ensures a high-performance collaboration where users seamlessly integrate into the brand's ecosystem.

The information exchange isn't a one-way street; it's a continuous, reciprocal loop where both parties contribute to the evolving narrative. Users, armed with precise brand knowledge, act as informed advocates, defenders, and contributors, elevating the brand's presence in the digital landscape.

As knowledge becomes the currency that fuels this transformative relationship, the shift from consumer to team member becomes more than a symbolic gesture.

It becomes a practical, real-time collaboration where information is not just shared but actively shapes the trajectory of the brand.

Brands, directed by Maslow's Pyramid, become heroes of the people.

In the Personing era, brand knowledge isn't static—it's a living, breathing entity that propels both brands and users forward in a journey of mutual growth and understanding.

Empowering Through Information

The real-time, high-performance information feedback loop serves as a powerful tool in the collaborative evolution of design for agile brands.

Users, armed with immediate insights and nuanced understanding, become integral contributors to the design process.

Their feedback, derived from the ongoing interaction within the Personing framework, shapes products and services in real-time, ensuring they align closely with user needs and expectations.

Agile Iterations and Rapid Improvements

The deconstruction and reconstruction of industrial value chains is an inevitable step.

For the most agile brands, the information loop becomes a mechanism for agile iterations and rapid improvements.

It goes beyond the conventional design phases, allowing brands to adapt swiftly to emerging trends, preferences, and challenges.

The immediacy of user feedback ensures that brands can make real-time adjustments, enhancing the user experience and staying at the forefront of innovation.

Enhanced User-Centric Approaches

The high-performance information feedback loop transforms brands into entities that prioritize user-centric approaches.

It provides brands with a direct line to user experiences, preferences, and pain points.

This knowledge becomes the cornerstone for designing products and services that not only meet but exceed user expectations.

The result is a more empathetic and responsive brand that evolves in tandem with its user community.

The goal is for a brand to grow human roots.

Dynamic Responsiveness to Market Shifts

In the fast-paced landscape of the Personing era, brands equipped with a real-time information feedback loop exhibit dynamic responsiveness to market shifts.

This agility allows them to adapt quickly to changing consumer behaviors, industry trends, and competitive landscapes.

By tapping into the collective intelligence of their user-base, brands can stay ahead of the curve, ensuring that their products and services remain relevant and desirable.

As brands embrace the power of real-time, high-performance information feedback loops, they not only strengthen the bond with their users but also enhance their design processes.

The collaborative evolution of products and services becomes a testament to the agility and responsiveness that define success in the Personing era.

It's a journey where brands and users co-create, iterate, and innovate, ensuring that each product or service is a reflection of the dynamic interplay between the brand and its engaged community.

The Educator's Role in the Trust Economy

In the trust economy of Personing, educators play a pivotal role as facilitators of informed decision-making.

Their responsibility extends beyond traditional knowledge transfer; educators become guides who empower individuals with the critical thinking skills necessary to navigate the complex landscape of trust and authenticity in the digital age.

Nurturing Critical Thinking and Media Literacy

Educators become champions of critical thinking and media literacy, equipping individuals with the tools to discern trustworthy information from the noise.

In a world saturated with data and messages, the educator's role is to instill a discerning mindset, enabling learners to question, analyze, and validate information sources, fostering a generation of savvy and discerning consumers. This discerning skill is paramount for people to stay relevant and above the onslaught of AI circumvolutions.

Empowering the Human Trust Interface

The educator's mission extends to empowering the human trust interface.

By instilling values of empathy, ethical decision-making, and transparency, educators contribute to the development of individuals who, as active participants in the trust economy, can engage in meaningful, authentic interactions.

This emphasis on human-centric skills ensures that the trust built is not just transactional but forms the foundation for lasting, meaningful connections.

Cultivating Digital Citizenship and Ethical Behavior

In the digital age, educators become cultivators of digital citizenship and ethical behavior.

They guide individuals in navigating the online landscape responsibly, teaching the importance of ethical interactions, digital etiquette, and responsible information sharing.

Through this guidance, educators mold a generation that contributes positively to the digital discourse, fostering an environment where trust is earned and sustained.

As educators take on these multifaceted roles, they become architects of a trust economy where individuals are not only informed but empowered to participate in a human-centric, authentic exchange.

The educator's impact ripples beyond the classroom, shaping a society where trust is cultivated, values are upheld, and individuals are equipped to navigate the intricacies of the evolving trust landscape in the Personing era.

With all that said, we must also be aware of the ensuing debate:

On one hand, we have the argument that brands gain agility and relevance by leveraging the collective intelligence, empathy, and creativity of their user-base. This approach allows brands to tap into the vast pool of knowledge and insights that their users possess, enabling them to create more engaging, intuitive, and personalized products and experiences. By incorporating user-generated content and feedback into their strategies, brands can foster stronger connections with their audience, ultimately driving growth and success.

On the other hand, some might argue that relying too heavily on the collective intelligence of users could lead to a loss of brand identity and direction.

After all, if a brand is constantly changing its course based on the whims of its users, it may struggle to maintain a consistent message and vision. Additionally, there's the risk of "groupthink," where the desire for consensus and harmony within the user community could stifle innovation and creativity.

As we navigate the landscape of Personing and knowledge management, the fusion of historical successes, contemporary strategies, and future possibilities unfolds.

Brands must strike a delicate balance between harnessing the power of collective intelligence and maintaining their unique identity and vision.

By doing so, they can create a synergistic relationship with their users, leveraging their collective intelligence to drive innovation and relevance while staying true to their core values and mission.

Personing Ecosystem

Personing ecosystem refers to the interconnected network of individuals, organizations, and communities that participate in and contribute to the practice of Personing—the paradigm of trust-building and authentic communication between people. Overall, the Personing ecosystem represents a dynamic and evolving landscape where individuals and organizations collaborate to build genuine connections, foster trust, and create positive impact within their communities and beyond.

Brands to Bonds

Brands to Bonds

6

The Personing Revolution

The Personing Revolution marks the dawn of a new era where the rigid structures of branding give way to a more fluid, authentic, and human-centric approach.

Brands are no longer distant entities projecting carefully curated images; they are living, breathing entities that engage, evolve, and resonate within the pulse of their engaged communities.

This paradigm shift ushers in a narrative where the power dynamic between brands and individuals undergoes a profound transformation.

From Providers to Champions

At the heart of The Personing Revolution lies the evolution of brands from providers into champions of the people.

It's a departure from transactional relationships to a realm where brands actively champion the needs, aspirations, and values of their engaged communities.

Personing is not just a strategy; it's a declaration that brands are not here merely to sell – they are here to empathize, understand, and stand alongside their audience.

Authenticity in Action

Personing is authenticity in action.

It's a declaration that the era of artificial constructs and glossy facades is giving way to a more genuine, transparent, and open dialogue.

Brands embracing *The Personing Revolution* embark on a journey where authenticity is not just a buzzword but a guiding principle. It's an acknowledgment that the true power of a brand lies not in its image but in its ability to connect authentically with the people it serves.

As we delve into *The Personing Revolution*, we unravel a narrative where brands become more than providers of products or services; they become integral parts of the communities they serve.

This revolution is not just about changing strategies; it's about rewriting the narrative of brand-consumer relationships, forging connections that are deeper, more meaningful, and enduring.

The Personing Revolution invites brands to step into a realm where they are not just champions of products or services – they are champions of the people.

Case Simulations

1. Empathy-Driven E-commerce

Challenge: A traditional e-commerce giant faced challenges in retaining customer loyalty amid fierce competition.

Personing Approach: The brand transitioned from a transactional platform to an empathetic community hub. They integrated real-time feedback loops, actively listened to customer concerns, and personalized interactions. This shift resulted in increased customer satisfaction, loyalty, and a community-driven marketplace where users felt heard and valued.

Next Level: Personing Corporate Officer manages real time flow of input and packages them into real time supply impacting daily decision making upon the production chain.

2. Authentic Food Delivery

Challenge: A popular food delivery service struggled with a generic brand image in a saturated market.

Personing Approach: The brand redefined itself by embracing Personing principles.

They highlighted local cuisines, engaged with users on social media, and empowered delivery partners as integral members. This human-centric approach led to a surge in orders, positive brand sentiment, and a genuine connection with users and partners alike.

Next Level: Personing Manager uses AI model to pool and redirect daily customer conversation feedback into management to improve daily decision making upon production.

3. Personal Finance Reinvented

Challenge: A traditional financial institution faced skepticism and low engagement in the digital age.

Personing Approach: The institution shifted from a purely transactional model to a financial wellness partner. They provided educational content, engaged in open dialogues about financial concerns, and personalized services based on individual needs. This transition resulted in increased trust, customer retention, and a perception shift from a faceless institution to a trusted financial ally.

Next Level: Personing Feedback Platform inputs daily conversation feedback into financial product placing model to discover micro-niches of urgent financial needs.

4. Health and Wellness Community

Challenge: A fitness app struggled with user churn and a lack of community engagement.

Personing Approach: The app rebranded itself as a wellness community. They introduced live workout sessions, facilitated user interactions, and shared authentic stories of personal transformations. The result was a thriving community, increased user retention, and a shift from a mere fitness app to a supportive wellness ecosystem.

Next Level: Personing Manager redirects success cases towards awareness and engagement of community related issues that are supportive of healthy lifestyles.

5. Sustainable Fashion Movement

Challenge: A fashion brand faced criticism for its environmental impact and lack of transparency.

Personing Approach: The brand embraced sustainability as a core value. They shared transparent insights into their supply chain, collaborated with eco-conscious influencers, and actively promoted responsible fashion practices. This Personing strategy led to an increase in eco-friendly product sales, positive media coverage, and a community of conscious consumers.

Next Level: Personing Corporate Officer redirects daily feedback from customers into direct action programs designed to positively impact communities in need of social and economic development.

These case simulations illustrate the transformative power of Personing, where brands evolve from providers to champions, fostering authentic connections, and creating value beyond transactions.

Overcoming Challenges in Transition

Transitioning from a profit-at-any-cost approach to the profitable Personing approach is a significant paradigm shift that involves overcoming various challenges.

Here, we present a list of protocols that guide brands through this transformative journey, ensuring a smooth evolution into a community-building, human-centric entity.

Embrace Transparency Gradually

Challenge: The fear of exposing vulnerabilities and imperfections can hinder the shift to Personing.

Protocol: Start by gradually embracing transparency. Share success stories, showcase behind-the-scenes processes, and address challenges openly. This gradual approach builds trust without overwhelming the audience.

Foster Internal Cultural Shift

Challenge: Employees accustomed to a transactional mindset may struggle with the shift to community-centric values.

Protocol: Prioritize internal communication and cultural shifts. Engage employees in the vision of Personing, provide training on empathy-driven interactions.

And create a culture where team members feel empowered to contribute to the community-building ethos.

Establish a Robust Feedback Loop

Challenge: Establishing a real-time feedback loop may seem daunting for brands accustomed to one-way communication.

Protocol: Invest in technology that enables real-time feedback. Actively listen to customer concerns, analyze feedback data, and use insights to adapt strategies. Make customers feel heard by implementing visible changes based on their input.

Educate Stakeholders on Personing Principles

Challenge: External stakeholders, such as investors and partners, may resist a shift that appears to prioritize community over profit.

Protocol: Develop educational materials and sessions to communicate the long-term benefits of Personing. Showcase how building a community leads to sustainable profitability, customer loyalty, and positive brand equity.

Personalize Without Overstepping Boundaries

Challenge: Balancing personalization with privacy concerns is a delicate challenge.

Protocol: Implement a thoughtful personalization strategy. Seek user consent for data usage, be transparent about data practices, and focus on delivering personalized experiences that enhance rather than invade privacy.

Align Marketing Strategies with Personing Values

Challenge: Traditional marketing strategies may not align with the authentic, community-driven ethos of Personing.

Protocol: Revise marketing strategies to align with Personing principles. Prioritize storytelling, community engagement, and values-driven content over aggressive sales tactics. Showcase the brand's commitment to community well-being and long-term community goals, instead of simply responding to the immediate needs. Again, marketing strategies must be redesigned from the bottom of Maslow's Pyramid and up, to become a partner of the journey of the people.

Continuously Evolve Based on Feedback

Challenge: The temptation to revert to old transactional methods may arise in the face of initial resistance or challenges.

Protocol: Stay committed to continuous evolution based on feedback. Regularly reassess strategies, analyze results, and be open to tweaking approaches. The Personing journey is dynamic, requiring adaptability and a willingness to learn from ongoing experiences.

By following these protocols, brands can navigate the challenges of transitioning to Personing successfully. The protocol emphasizes a gradual and thoughtful approach, ensuring that the evolution is not only profitable but also aligned with the values of community, transparency, and authenticity.

Future Lessons from Early Adopters

As brands embark on the transformative journey of adopting Personing principles, early adopters will serve as pioneers, offering valuable insights and lessons for those following in their footsteps.

By studying the experiences of these trailblazers, we will project several key lessons that are likely to shape the evolution of Personing in the business landscape.

Authenticity as a Currency

Early adopters will demonstrate that authenticity is not just a buzzword; it's a tangible currency that builds trust and loyalty.

Brands that genuinely embrace transparency, will share authentic narratives, and admit imperfections garner stronger connections with their communities.

Community-Centric Decision-Making

Successful early adopters will showcase the importance of involving the community in decision-making processes.

Brands that actively seek and incorporate user feedback, will become leaders in co-creating with their community, and consider the collective voice in strategic decisions experience heightened engagement and loyalty.

Balancing Profitability and Purpose

Lessons from early adopters indicate that profitability and purpose are not mutually exclusive.

Brands that align their profit goals with a genuine commitment to community well-being find that a purpose-driven approach not only resonates with users but also contributes to sustainable profitability.

Empathy-Driven Innovation

The early adopter experience emphasizes the role of empathy in driving innovation.

Brands that prioritize understanding user needs, concerns, and aspirations can innovate products and services that truly resonate with their audience, fostering a sense of shared purpose and collaboration.

Continuous Adaptability

Early adopters will underscore the importance of continuous evolution.

Brands that remain agile, adapt based on feedback, and stay attuned to the evolving needs of their community are more likely to thrive in the Personing paradigm.

Humanizing Technology

As technology plays a significant role in Personing strategies, early adopters teach us the importance of humanizing technology.

Brands that use technology as an enabler for authentic human connections, rather than a replacement, find success in creating meaningful interactions.

Educating Stakeholders

Successful Personing adopters will recognize the need to educate internal and external stakeholders on the principles and benefits of Personing.

Lessons indicate that a collective understanding and commitment to Personing principles at all levels of the organization will contribute to smoother transitions.

Measuring Beyond Transactions

Early adopters will highlight the shift from measuring success solely through transactions to evaluating broader metrics such as community engagement, sentiment, and advocacy.

Brands that redefine success metrics in the Personing era will gain a more comprehensive understanding of their impact.

Building a Resilient Brand Ecosystem

The Personing journey is not just about the brand but the entire ecosystem it operates within.

Early adopters show the importance of building resilient brand ecosystems that foster collaboration, mutual support, and a shared sense of purpose among all stakeholders.

As more brands join the Personing revolution, these early adopter lessons provide a roadmap for navigating challenges, fostering genuine connections, and creating a business landscape where brands become champions of the people.

The evolving narrative of Personing will be shaped by these pioneers, offering a wealth of lessons for those who embrace the transformative power of authentic, community-driven interactions.

In this dynamic and ever-changing landscape, brands must be like the Energizer Bunny of the business world, constantly adapting and evolving to stay ahead of the curve.

Brands to Bonds

Social Isolation

Social isolation refers to a state in which individuals lack meaningful social connections or interactions with others, leading to feelings of loneliness, disconnection, and alienation. It can occur both physically, through limited contact with others, and emotionally, through a sense of detachment or exclusion from social networks. Social isolation can occur for various reasons, including geographic location, life transitions, disability, illness, or socioeconomic factors. Addressing social isolation requires interventions at individual, community, and societal levels to promote social connections, foster supportive relationships, and build inclusive communities.

Brands to Bonds

Brands to Bonds

7
Building Bonds in the AI Age

We now face the dazzling rocketry of rapid technological advancement, where Artificial Intelligence (AI) is weaving its way into the fabric of our daily lives and the essence of human connection stands at a critical crossroad.

As algorithms analyze data and bots handle routine tasks, there's a risk of losing the profound beauty that comes from genuine human interactions.

Yet, amidst the surge of AI, the call for building bonds echoes louder than ever.

The Paradox of Progress

As AI evolves to perform complex tasks and streamline processes, there's an inherent paradox unfolding.

While technology propels us into a future of unparalleled efficiency, it also threatens to distance us from the warmth of human touch.

It's against this backdrop that the significance of consciously building bonds in the AI age emerges.

Surely this could lead to our greatest time yet.

AI as a Catalyst, Not a Replacement

AI, at its core, should be viewed as a catalyst rather than a replacement for human connection.

It's a tool that, when wielded mindfully, can amplify our ability to understand, empathize, and connect on a deeper level.

Building bonds in the AI age is not a retreat from technology but a strategic embrace, ensuring that progress doesn't come at the cost of authentic human relationships.

Unveiling the Human Trust Interface

In this chapter, we delve into the art and science of Building Bonds in the AI Age.

We explore how the very technology designed to streamline our lives can be harnessed to fortify, rather than erode, the foundations of human connection.

Central to this exploration is the concept of the Human Trust Interface – a space where AI and human interactions harmonize to create an environment where bonds are not just sustained but strengthened.

The Journey of Personing Continues

As we navigate the terrain of the AI age, the journey of Personing evolves. It's a journey that beckons us to be architects of a future where technology serves humanity, rather than overshadowing it.

The call to build bonds is a call to infuse technology with the essence of our shared humanity, ensuring that progress doesn't come at the expense of the profound connections that define us.

So, let's embark on this exploration, discovering the nuanced dance between AI and human bonds, and redefining what it means to truly connect in the age of artificial intelligence.

Community Building Through Personing

Personing in the AI age is rooted in authentic storytelling. Brands and individuals alike become storytellers, weaving narratives that resonate with the human experience.

By sharing genuine stories, vulnerabilities, and triumphs, a community forms around shared values, fostering a sense of belonging.

Collaborative Innovation

The AI age invites collaborative innovation through Personing.

Community members, whether customers or collaborators, are not passive entities but active contributors.

Brands involve their communities in co-creating, ideating, and shaping the products and services, turning consumers into valued partners in the journey.

Human-Centric Technology

Personing transcends the dichotomy of humans versus technology.

In community building, technology becomes a facilitator for deeper connections.

AI is utilized not to replace but to enhance human interactions.

Chatbots offer real-time support, algorithms personalize experiences, and analytics predict community needs, all while maintaining the human touch.

Not just cold numbers, but deep feelings.

Empathy-Driven Interactions

The cornerstone of community building through Personing is empathy.

In the AI age, technology is employed to understand and respond to the emotional nuances of community members.

Brands leverage data not just for personalization but to genuinely comprehend the needs, concerns, and joys of their community, fostering a culture of empathy.

So that, in times of joy, brands celebrate along their partners, and in times of crisis, brands thrown everything away and embrace people.

Dynamic Engagement Platforms

Personing advocates for dynamic engagement platforms where the community actively participates.

From interactive forums and live Q&A sessions to immersive virtual experiences, the AI age provides a myriad of tools to create vibrant, two-way communication.

The community is not a passive audience but an engaged participant in the brand's journey.

Continuous Learning and Adaptation

The AI age unfolds with rapid advancements, and Personing necessitates a commitment to continuous learning.

Community building is not a static process but an evolving journey.

Brands and individuals alike must stay attuned to the changing dynamics, adapting strategies to meet the evolving needs and expectations of the community.

Shared Values and Purpose

The foundation of community building in the AI age lies in shared values and purpose.

Personing principles guide the alignment of brand values with those of the community. This alignment fosters a sense of purpose that transcends transactions, creating a community where individuals feel connected *to something larger than themselves.*

As we navigate the complexities of the AI age, community building through Personing emerges as a transformative force, demonstrating that technology and human connection are not mutually exclusive.

It's a journey that invites us to harness the power of AI to amplify our ability to connect authentically, creating communities that thrive in the delicate balance between innovation and humanity.

Adapting to Personing Feedback

In the ever-evolving landscape of Personing in the AI age, the ability to adapt to change and embrace feedback becomes paramount.

This section explores the dynamic interplay between adaptation, feedback loops, and the continuous evolution required to thrive in a community-centric environment enriched by the integration of AI.

Embracing Evolution

Personing calls for a mindset that embraces *evolution as a constant*. Brands and individuals navigating the AI age must be agile and open to evolving strategies, approaches, and even core values based on the ever-changing dynamics of the community and technological landscape.

Feedback as a Catalyst for Improvement

Feedback, rather than being perceived as criticism, is a catalyst for improvement.

In the AI age, technology facilitates real-time feedback loops that allow brands to understand community sentiments, preferences, and concerns swiftly. This data becomes a valuable resource for iterative enhancements and innovations.

Agile Decision-Making

Agile decision-making is a cornerstone of thriving in the AI-infused Personing era.

The ability to process feedback swiftly, make data-informed decisions, and implement changes with speed ensures that brands stay responsive to community needs and remain resilient in the face of evolving challenges.

Inclusive Co-Creation

The AI age introduces the concept of inclusive co-creation, where feedback is not only received but actively sought.

Brands invite the community into the creative process, encouraging collaboration and ensuring that the products, services, and experiences are shaped by the collective wisdom of the community.

Adapting Technology Ethically

As technology evolves, ethical considerations become crucial.

Adapting to change involves not only embracing technological advancements but doing so ethically.

Brands must navigate the ethical implications of AI, ensuring that the integration of technology aligns with community values and respects privacy and transparency.

Learning from Negative Feedback

Negative feedback, rather than being feared, is seen as an opportunity for growth.

Understanding the nuances of dissatisfaction provides valuable insights into areas that need improvement.

Brands that learn from negative feedback and transparently address concerns demonstrate a commitment to the community's well-being.

Strategic Iteration

Strategic iteration becomes a key operational principle.

Personing in the AI age involves an ongoing cycle of planning, implementation, feedback analysis, and strategic adjustments.

This iterative approach ensures that brands stay attuned to the pulse of the community, fostering a culture of continuous improvement.

As we navigate the dynamic intersection of Personing, AI, and community building, adapting to change and feedback emerges not as a challenge but as a guiding principle.

It's a commitment to an ongoing journey of improvement, co-creation, and ethical use of technology, creating a harmonious dance between human-centric values and the transformative potential of AI.

Dynamic Relationships Over Time

As we visualize the intricate tapestry of Personing within the AI age, we discover that relationships are not static but dynamic, evolving entities.

This section delves into the nuanced nature of relationships over time, exploring the ways in which Personing principles, combined with AI integration, shape and deepen connections within the community.

Building Trust Through Consistency

Consistency forms the bedrock of trust-building in dynamic relationships. Brands and individuals practicing Personing aim for a consistent presence, message, and values over time. This unwavering commitment to authenticity and reliability fosters a sense of trust within the community.

The Evolution of Community Roles

Personing acknowledges that community roles are not fixed but evolve.

Over time, community members transition from passive consumers to active contributors and collaborators.

The relationship dynamic shifts, reflecting a journey where individuals become integral participants in the co-creation of the brand narrative.

Responsive Adaptation to Community Needs

Dynamic relationships thrive on responsiveness to changing community needs.

Personing leverages AI to gather real-time insights into evolving preferences, expectations, and concerns. Brands that adapt their strategies and offerings based on this dynamic feedback demonstrate a commitment to staying attuned to the community's pulse.

Nurturing Emotional Connections

The AI age introduces tools for nurturing emotional connections over time. Personing emphasizes the role of technology in understanding and responding to the emotional nuances of community members.

AI-driven personalization ensures that interactions evoke emotional resonance, deepening the bonds between the brand and the community.

Storytelling as a Continuous Thread

Storytelling acts as a continuous thread weaving through the fabric of dynamic relationships.

Brands tell stories that evolve, reflecting the collective experiences, triumphs, and challenges of the community. This ongoing narrative creates a sense of continuity, anchoring the community in a shared journey.

Predictive Personalization for Long-Term Engagement

Personing leverages AI for predictive personalization, anticipating the long-term engagement needs of the community.

Algorithms analyze historical data to forecast preferences, allowing brands to tailor experiences and offerings that align with the evolving expectations of community members over time.

Cultivating a Culture of Appreciation

In dynamic relationships, a culture of appreciation becomes vital.

Personing encourages brands to continuously express gratitude, acknowledge contributions, and celebrate milestones within the community.

This culture of appreciation nurtures a positive environment and reinforces the mutual value in the ongoing relationship.

As we navigate the ebb and flow of dynamic relationships within the AI-infused Personing landscape, it becomes clear that longevity is not merely about time but about the depth of connection forged over that time.

Personing principles, when blended with the capabilities of AI, lay the foundation for relationships that evolve, adapt, and flourish in the ever-changing currents of the community and technological evolution.

In the age of AI overlords *(though let's be honest, they're probably still working on folding laundry),* connecting with people takes more than just catchy slogans and pixel-perfect influencers. It's all about Personing, which basically means ditching the robot suit and showing your human side.

Can we push on imagination, please???

Say, a toothpaste brand that, instead of blinding you with CGI smiles, tells the story of their CEO's lifelong struggle with rogue popcorn kernels getting stuck in their teeth in front of his girlfriend!

Or a fitness guru who confesses on X that their pre-workout ritual involves frantic Googling *"more honest reasons to exercise besides looking good in a swimsuit."*

Vulnerability is the new six-pack!

This authentic storytelling creates a community around shared experiences. It's realizing your neighbor also hoards slightly-expired coupons - suddenly you're not alone in your quest for discount wasabi peas. It's finding your tribe, except instead of grunting around a fire, you're bonding over slightly embarrassing memes about AI taking over the world *(which, don't worry about it, definitely not gonna happen... nervous laughter...)*

So, the next time you're crafting a message, ditch the marketing jargon and unleash your inner weirdo.

Because let's face it, who can resist a brand that admits to having the same social anxiety as a houseplant?

Brands to Bonds

Fully Human Organization

A fully human organization is a workplace environment that prioritizes the holistic well-being, growth, and fulfillment of its employees, recognizing their humanity and individuality beyond their roles or contributions to the organization. Overall, a fully human organization recognizes that its greatest asset is its people and strives to create an environment where employees can thrive, contribute their best work, and find fulfillment in their professional and personal lives.

Brands to Bonds

Brands to Bonds

8

The Future of Trust: Personing as a Blucprint

The boundless expanse of the AI Age stands before us, with algorithms orchestrating symphonies of data and chatbots dancing through digital landscapes, with the future of trust emerging as a beacon amidst the technological tumult.

This chapter is a journey into the heart of this future – a future where Personing stands as a guiding light, illuminating the path towards genuine human connection in a world increasingly dominated by artificial intelligence.

As AI pervades communication, a fascinating paradox emerges: while technology automates interactions, *the human craving for genuine connection and trust intensifies.* From the depths of neural networks to the intricate web of human behavior, insights gleaned from the neural, behavior, and communication sciences paint a vivid picture of the future of trust.

As AI continues its march forward, transforming the way we communicate, transact, and interact, *the value of human trust shines brighter than ever before.*

In the midst of the robotization of communications, humans instinctively gravitate towards human trust as a beacon of authenticity in a sea of digital noise.

While AI may excel at simulating human-like interactions, it is the innate human ability to empathize, connect, and understand that ultimately fosters genuine trust and rapport.

Personing emerges as the blueprint for trust in the AI Age, offering a roadmap for navigating the complexities of human-AI interactions.

By infusing technology with humanity, Personing transcends the limitations of robotization, creating spaces where trust flourishes, relationships deepen, and communities thrive.

As we peer into the future, we glimpse a world where human trust reigns supreme, where the art of Personing transcends the artificial constructs of technology, and where authenticity, empathy, and connection become the currency of trust in the ever-evolving landscape of the AI Age.

Join us on this journey as we explore the future of trust, where Personing stands as a beacon of hope, guiding us towards a future where humanity triumphs over technology, and trust reigns supreme.

Drawing from neural, behavior, and communication sciences, here's an insight into the future of trust in the AI Age:

The Robotic Facade

AI-powered communication tools will become increasingly sophisticated, mimicking human speech and even emotions.

However, research suggests our brains readily differentiate between genuine human connection and simulated interactions.

Studies on mirror neurons, which fire when we observe actions or emotions, show they remain largely inactive during interaction with AI.

This suggests a fundamental human need for authentic emotional resonance, something AI may struggle to replicate.

The Trust Gap and the Empathy Edge

As AI handles routine communication tasks, humans will likely become more discerning, reserving trust for interactions that require empathy, understanding, and nuanced emotional intelligence.

Studies on the limbic system, our brain's emotional center, reveal it plays a crucial role in building trust.

AI, lacking this biological foundation, may face limitations in building deep trust relationships.

The Human Advantage

The very act of navigating the complexities of human communication, with its ambiguities and emotional nuances, may become a valued human skill.

Research on cultural and situational communication complexities highlights the challenges AI faces in adapting to diverse contexts. This adaptability, rooted in human experience and intuition, could become a key differentiator for human communicators.

Building Hybrid Trust Models

The future may lie in hybrid trust models, where AI augments human communication, handling rote tasks while humans focus on building genuine connections.

Imagine AI assistants gathering data and summarizing information, leaving space for human empathy and emotional intelligence to close the deal or offer meaningful support.

The Neural Imperative

Understanding Trust from the Inside Out:

As we design AI for communication, understanding the neural basis of trust becomes crucial.

Studying mirror neurons, the limbic system, and the always complex interplay of neurotransmitters during human interactions can inform the development of AI that fosters, rather than undermines, trust.

In conclusion, the robotization of communication will not diminish the value of human trust.

Instead, it might elevate it, making genuine human connection, empathy, and emotional intelligence even more sought-after.

By understanding the neural and behavioral underpinnings of trust, we can build AI systems that complement, rather than replace, the irreplaceable human touch in communication.

The future may not be about humans versus machines, but about humans and machines working together to build trust in a complex and ever-evolving world.

Personing and the Evolving Landscape

In the ever-evolving landscape of the AI Age, the quest for trust acquisition takes on new dimensions as humans navigate the intricate interplay between technology and humanity.

As humans grapple with the need for trust in an increasingly digital world, they turn to insights from neural sciences, behavioral psychology, and even explore the realm of psychic possibilities to train themselves in the art of Personing.

The Human Response to the Need for Trust in the AI Age

Humans, instinctively recognizing the inherent value of trust amidst the sea of artificial intelligence, respond to the need for trust acquisition with a blend of curiosity, adaptability, and resilience.

In the face of robotization of communications, they seek out solutions that resonate with their innate desire for authentic connections and genuine rapport.

Thus, empaths become masters of the future.

Insights from Neural Sciences

Drawing from insights gleaned from neural sciences, humans embark on a journey of self-discovery and skill development in trust acquisition.

They explore the neural pathways associated with empathy, intuition, and emotional intelligence, honing their ability to forge meaningful connections in the digital landscape.

Behavioral Psychology and the Art of Personing

Behavioral psychology serves as a guiding light in the art of Personing, offering valuable principles and techniques for building trust in the AI Age.

Humans delve into the nuances of human behavior, learning to navigate the intricacies of communication, persuasion, and relationship-building with finesse and grace.

The immediate consequence of this process is that humans realize that the knowledge of the true potential for communication is scarce, which will open urgent research into areas previously thought of as unnecessary.

Exploring Psychic Field Possibilities

In their quest for trust acquisition, humans explore the far-reaching possibilities of the psychic field, tapping into intuitive insights, telepathic connections, and energetic resonance.

They recognize that trust transcends mere words and actions, extending into the realm of energetic exchange and subtle vibrations.

So it would not be too far fetched to revisit the potential implications for the retaking of unusual methodologies, today considered bordering on fringe and officially not sanctioned by science, such as Kirlian photography or radionics, as baseline to depart in this exploration.

As humans traverse the evolving landscape of the AI Age, they embrace the art of Personing as a beacon of authenticity, empathy, and connection in a world dominated by artificial intelligence.

Drawing from insights across neural sciences, behavioral psychology, and the psychic field, they embark on a journey of self-discovery and skill development, forging genuine connections that transcend the boundaries of technology and propel humanity towards a future where trust reigns supreme.

Emerging Trends in Human-Centric Commerce

In the dynamic intersection of technology and humanity, emerging trends in human-centric commerce are reshaping the way we interact, transact, and build trust in the AI Age.

Drawing from insights across neural sciences, behavioral psychology, and the exploration of psychic possibilities, these trends reflect a deepening commitment to authenticity, empathy, and connection in the digital landscape.

Authenticity as Currency

Authenticity emerges as the currency of human-centric commerce in the AI Age.

As humans seek genuine connections amidst the digital noise, brands that embrace the ripples of authenticity in their interactions, communications, and offerings begin to stand out and get ahead of those mired in status quo.

From transparent business practices to authentic storytelling, authenticity becomes the cornerstone of trust acquisition and brand loyalty.

Empathetic Engagement

Empathetic engagement takes center stage as brands prioritize understanding and responding to the emotional needs of their audience.

Drawing from insights from neural sciences, brands cultivate empathetic connections, recognizing and validating the emotions of their customers.

Through empathetic engagement, brands forge deep and lasting bonds built on trust and understanding.

Personalization with Purpose

Personalization evolves beyond mere data-driven algorithms to encompass a deeper sense of purpose.

In human-centric commerce, personalization is not just about targeting individuals based on their preferences, but about aligning offerings with their values, aspirations, and unique identities. Brands leverage insights from behavioral psychology to deliver personalized experiences that resonate on a profound level with their audience.

Community-Centric Approach

A community-centric approach emerges as a powerful trend in human-centric commerce, emphasizing the importance of fostering genuine connections and collaborative relationships within communities.

Brands recognize the value of building communities around shared interests, values, and experiences, creating spaces where individuals feel a sense of belonging and connection beyond transactions.

Integration of Human and Technological Touchpoints

The integration of human and technological touchpoints becomes increasingly prevalent in human-centric commerce.

While technology enhances efficiency and scale, humans remain at the heart of meaningful interactions and trust-building.

Brands strike a delicate balance between automation and human presence, leveraging technology to augment rather than replace human connections.

No more clients or users, but partners.

Evolving Ethics and Responsibility

Ethics and responsibility take on heightened significance in human-centric commerce.

Brands navigate very complex ethical considerations surrounding data privacy, algorithmic bias, and social responsibility with transparency and integrity.

They prioritize ethical practices that respect the dignity and autonomy of individuals, fostering trust and loyalty in the process. As human-centric commerce continues to evolve in the AI Age, these emerging trends underscore a fundamental shift towards authenticity, empathy, and connection. By embracing these trends, brands can navigate the complexities of the digital landscape while fostering genuine relationships, building trust, and creating meaningful value for their audience.

Predictions for the Next Decade

As we peer into the horizon of the next decade, the implementation of Personing in corporate structures heralds a seismic shift in executive operations and decision-making processes.

Here are some predictions for the future landscape:

Overhaul of Executive Structures

Corporate implementation of Personing necessitates a complete overhaul of executive structure. Traditional hierarchies give way to a more inclusive model, opening space among upper echelons for the arrival of brand partners as top directors of specific company operations.

These brand partners bring a wealth of consumer insights, direction input in product and service development, and a deep understanding of community needs.

Expect to see stay at home moms partnering grandly in product development feedback.

Improving Decision Making

Personing revolutionizes decision-making processes within companies. Real-time Open Source Intelligence (OSINT) becomes the norm, enabling organizations to gather insights from diverse sources and respond swiftly to changing market dynamics.

This transparent approach to information collection empowers brand partners to contribute directly to decision-making processes, fostering agility and innovation.

Real-Time Collaboration

Companies embrace real-time collaboration as a cornerstone of Personing.

Rather than relying on stealthy, undercover methods of information collection, organizations open channels for brand partners to contribute openly and directly.

Information flows freely through Personing communication infrastructure, providing decision-makers with real-time insights from the frontline at communities and shops.

Cultivating Trust through Transparency

Transparency becomes a core value in corporate operations. Instead of clandestine data collection practices that erode trust if exposed, companies adopt a transparent approach by inviting brand partners to share their insights openly.

This shift from spying to open collaboration cultivates trust and authenticity, enhancing the brand's reputation and prestige.

Empowering Brand Partners

Brand partners are empowered to become active participants in shaping company strategies and operations.

Rather than being passive consumers, they are invited to share their perspectives, preferences, and feedback openly. This empowerment not only strengthens the bond between brands and their communities but also fosters a sense of ownership and pride among brand partners.

Embracing the Personing Approach

Ultimately, the Personing approach transforms corporate culture, turning information gathering into a collaborative and prestigious endeavor.

Companies no longer need spying on our personal data. Instead, they invite brand friends to share what they need to know openly and directly.

By making Personing cool and prestigious, companies embrace a new era of trust, transparency, and community-centricity.

As we embark on the journey into the next decade, the implementation of Personing promises to revolutionize corporate operations, empower brand friends, and foster a culture of trust and collaboration.

By embracing this paradigm shift, companies can navigate the complexities of the digital age with authenticity, agility, and purpose, paving the way for a future where brands and communities thrive in harmony.

So, let the AI march on, its whirring gears and blinking lights a testament to human ingenuity.

But let us never forget the fragile, irreplaceable power of trust.

It's the secret ingredient that transforms cold transactions into meaningful connections, the bridge between the symphony of ones and zeros and the messy, beautiful symphony of humanity.

Brands to Bonds

Brands to Bonds

Paradigm Evolution

Paradigm evolution refers to the process by which fundamental beliefs, assumptions, and conceptual frameworks within a particular field or discipline undergo gradual or abrupt changes over time. It involves shifts in the prevailing worldview, guiding principles, and methodologies that shape how problems are perceived, understood, and addressed within the domain. Overall, paradigm evolution is a dynamic and iterative process characterized by the continuous refinement, transformation, and replacement of existing paradigms with new conceptual frameworks, theories, and methodologies that better capture the complexities of the world and advance understanding within the discipline.

Brands to Bonds

Brands to Bonds

9

Forging Enduring Bonds

Thus, at last we have come to the point where we must braid our arguments into the art of forging enduring bonds, in a celebration of the transformative power of Personing, where trust, empathy, and transparency converge to create relationships that transcend the transactional and endure through time.

As we journey through the intricacies of Personing, we witness the profound impact it has on the way brands engage with their communities, and the way individuals connect with one another.

From the foundational principles of authenticity and empathy to the strategic integration of technology and humanity, Personing offers a blueprint for building relationships that stand the test of time.

Through the lens of trust, we explore how Personing fosters authentic connections built on transparency and integrity.

By inviting brand friends into the decision-making process and embracing real-time collaboration, organizations cultivate a culture of trust that resonates with their communities.

Empathy emerges as a guiding force in the art of forging enduring bonds.

Personing encourages brands to listen, understand, and respond to the emotional needs of their audience, creating spaces where individuals feel valued, heard, and respected.

This empathetic engagement fosters deep and meaningful connections that transcend mere transactions.

As we navigate the evolving landscape of human-centric commerce, we witness the strategic integration of technology and humanity in the pursuit of enduring bonds.

From personalized experiences to community-centric approaches, Personing leverages the power of AI to augment, rather than replace, human connections, ensuring that authenticity remains at the heart of every interaction.

Join us on this journey as we explore the transformative potential of Personing in forging enduring bonds that transcend the digital noise and resonate with the timeless essence of human connection.

Through trust, empathy, and authenticity, we unlock the true power of Personing to create relationships that stand the test of time.

Farewell to marketers! Long live the empaths, new masters of branding!

Key Concepts

As we conclude our exploration of Personing and its impact on trust acquisition and relationship building in the AI Age, let us revisit some of the key concepts that have emerged throughout this journey:

Authenticity as the Cornerstone

Authenticity lies at the heart of Personing, serving as the cornerstone upon which genuine connections are built. By embracing transparency, honesty, and integrity, brands cultivate trust and loyalty among their communities, fostering relationships that endure through time.

Empathy and Understanding

Empathy emerges as a guiding force in the art of forging enduring bonds. By listening, understanding, and responding to the emotional needs of their audience, brands create spaces where individuals feel valued, heard, and respected. This empathetic engagement fosters deep and meaningful connections that transcend mere transactions.

Strategic Integration of Technology and Humanity

Personing leverages the power of AI to augment, rather than replace, human connections.

Through the strategic integration of technology and humanity, brands create personalized experiences, community-centric approaches, and real-time collaboration that resonate with their audience on a profound level.

Trust through Transparency and Collaboration

Trust is cultivated through transparency and collaboration in the Personing approach.

By inviting brand partners into the decision-making process, embracing real-time collaboration, and fostering open communication channels, organizations build a culture of trust that resonates with their communities.

By integrating community representatives into the executive echelons of strategic direction as trusted feedback, brands advance into the heart of the human experience.

Enduring Bonds that Transcend Transactions

Ultimately, Personing is about forging enduring bonds that transcend the transactional and endure through time.

By prioritizing authenticity, empathy, and trust, brands create relationships that stand the test of time, resonating with the timeless essence of human connection. As we reflect on these key concepts, we recognize the transformative potential of Personing in reshaping the way brands engage with their communities and the way individuals connect with one another. Through trust, empathy, and authenticity, we unlock the true power of Personing to create relationships that inspire, empower, and endure.

The Personing Imperative

In the ever-evolving landscape of commerce, the imperative of Personing emerges as a transformative force, emphasizing the importance of *transformation over transaction* in the acquisition of trust. Personing transcends the traditional transactional approach to relationship building, ushering in a new era of authenticity, empathy, and connection.

At its core, Personing recognizes that trust is not simply acquired through a series of transactions, but rather through meaningful interactions, genuine engagement, and empathetic understanding.

It challenges the notion that trust can be bought or sold, and instead emphasizes the importance of building relationships based on mutual respect, transparency, and integrity.

By prioritizing transformation over transaction, Personing shifts the focus from short-term gains to long-term relationships.

It recognizes that true trust is cultivated over time, through consistent actions, open communication, and a commitment to understanding the needs and aspirations of individuals.

Personing also challenges the traditional power dynamics inherent in brand-consumer relationships.

Rather than positioning brands as distant entities to be admired from afar, Personing invites brands to become active participants in the lives of their audience, fostering genuine connections and building trust through shared experiences. The result is brands built by partners, not designers.

Furthermore, Personing acknowledges the importance of empathy in the acquisition of trust.

It recognizes that individuals are not just consumers, but complex beings with emotions, aspirations, and values.

By listening, understanding, and responding to the emotional needs of their audience, brands can create spaces where individuals feel valued, heard, and respected.

In essence, the imperative of Personing lies in its ability to foster enduring bonds that transcend the transactional.

It recognizes that trust is not a commodity to be bought or sold, but rather a precious asset to be nurtured and cultivated over time.

By prioritizing transformation, empathy, and authenticity, Personing paves the way for a future where relationships are built on mutual trust, respect, and understanding.

The big hit of this results in brands transitioning from a designer/director podium into a receiver/performer receptive stance that gradually dissolves the client/user paradigm in favor of a grand human partnership strategic approach.

A Clarion Call to Trust-Focused Professionals

To all trust-focused professionals navigating the ever-changing landscape of commerce and communication, the time has come to embrace the transformative power of Personing.

As champions of authenticity, empathy, and connection, you play a vital role in shaping the future of trust acquisition and relationship building in the AI Age.

We call upon you to join us in championing the Personing approach—a paradigm shift that prioritizes transformation over transaction, empathy over exploitation, and authenticity over artifice.

Together, we have the opportunity to revolutionize the way brands engage with their communities and the way individuals connect with one another.

As trust-focused professionals, you possess the skills, insights, and passion to lead this charge.

Your commitment to transparency, integrity, and empathy serves as a beacon of hope in an increasingly digital and disconnected world.

By embracing the principles of Personing, you have the power to inspire, empower, and transform the relationships between brands and their audience.

Let us come together to cultivate a culture of trust—one built on open communication, genuine engagement, and mutual respect.

Let us leverage the tools and technologies at our disposal to foster meaningful connections and build relationships that stand the test of time.

In the journey ahead, let us remain steadfast in our commitment to trust-focused practices, empathy-driven strategies, and authentic engagement.

Let us lead by example, demonstrating the transformative potential of Personing in reshaping the future of commerce and communication.

Together, as trust-focused professionals, we can create a world where trust is not just a commodity to be bought or sold, but a precious asset to be nurtured and cherished.

Join us in embracing the imperative of Personing, and together, let us build a future where relationships are built on trust, empathy, and real human authenticity.

Brands to Bonds

Courage of Vulnerability

The courage of vulnerability refers to the willingness to embrace and express one's authentic self, even in the face of uncertainty, risk, or emotional exposure. It involves acknowledging and accepting one's vulnerabilities, insecurities, and imperfections without fear of judgment or rejection. Instead of hiding behind masks of strength or perfection, individuals who embody the courage of vulnerability cultivate openness, honesty, and authenticity in their interactions and relationships. The courage of vulnerability is not about seeking perfection or avoiding discomfort, but rather about embracing the messy, imperfect, and authentic aspects of life with courage, compassion, and resilience. It empowers individuals to live wholeheartedly, connect authentically with others, and cultivate deeper meaning and fulfillment in their lives.

Brands to Bonds

Brands to Bonds

Brands to Bonds

References

Brown, Brene. "Daring Greatly: How the Courage to Be Vulnerable Transforms the Way We Live, Love, Parent, and Lead." Avery, 2012.

Cialdini, Robert B. "Influence: The Psychology of Persuasion." Harper Business, Revised edition, 2006.

Dammann, Olaf. "The Essence of Authenticity." Olaf Dammann, 1st edition, 2nd edition, 3rd edition.

Friederichs, Katja M. "The Essence of Authenticity." Katja M. Friederichs, 1st edition, 4th edition.

Lebedinski, Sabine. "The Essence of Authenticity." Sabine Lebedinski, 1st edition, 5th edition.

Liesenfeld, Kerstin M. "The Essence of Authenticity." Kerstin M. Liesenfeld, 1st edition, 2nd edition.

Goleman, Daniel. "Emotional Intelligence: Why It Can Matter More Than IQ." Bantam Books, 1995.

Kahneman, Daniel. "Thinking, Fast and Slow." Farrar, Straus and Giroux, 2011.

Pink, Daniel H. "To Sell Is Human: The Surprising Truth About Moving Others." Riverhead Books, Reprint edition, 2013.

Rogers, Carl R. "On Becoming a Person: A Therapist's View of Psychotherapy." Mariner Books, Reprint edition, 1995.

Ruskoff, Douglas. "Team Human." W. W. Norton & Company, 2019.

Twenge, Jean M. "iGen: Why Today's Super-Connected Kids Are Growing Up Less Rebellious, More Tolerant, Less Happy--and Completely Unprepared for Adulthood--and What That Means for the Rest of Us." Atria Books, Reprint edition, 2018.

Vaynerchuk, Gary. "Crushing It!: How Great Entrepreneurs Build Their Business and Influence-and How You Can, Too." Harper Business, Reprint edition, 2018.

Whitelaw, Sarah. "How to Be Yourself: Quiet Your Inner Critic and Rise Above Social Anxiety." The Experiment, 2018.

These references provide a comprehensive understanding of the psychological, behavioral, sociological, and business aspects underlying the concepts discussed in *"Brands to Bonds: The Evolution of Trust in the Age of AI."*

Brands to Bonds

Brands to Bonds

Work registered by Daniel Cruz, Toronto, Canada. This book is sold on the condition that it not be loaned, rented or otherwise distributed, commercially or by any other means, in any form of binding or cover other than that in which it is published. No part of this publication may be reproduced, stored in a retrieval system, or transmitted in any form or by any means (electronic, mechanical, photocopying, recording, or otherwise) without the prior written permission of Daniel Cruz.

© 2024 Daniel Cruz - All Rights Reserved

www.ingramcontent.com/pod-product-compliance
Lightning Source LLC
Chambersburg PA
CBHW031621210526
45464CB00004B/1679